FIRM FOUNDATIONS

CREATION TO CHRIST

BOOK 1

CHRONOLOGIAL TEACHING: WHY AND HOW

TREVOR MCILWAIN

First Printing 2009

Firm Foundations Creation to Christ (Revised Edition)
        Book 1: Chronological Teaching: Why and How
Copyright 2009 by   New Tribes Mission
                              1000 East First Street
                              Sanford, FL 32771-1487

ISBN Number: 1-890040-83-5

Printed in the United States of America

IMPORTANT

Cross-cultural teaching

For teaching rural ethnic people or tribal groups, this curriculum's companion series, *Building on Firm Foundations*, is more suitable and highly recommended.

Order information

Australia: books_aus@ntm.org **or** 07.3208.9634
Canada: www.ntmc.ca **or** bookstore@ntmc.ca **or** 519.369.2622
United Kingdom: http://uk.ntm.org/shop **or** books@ntm.org.uk **or** 44.1472.387700
USA: www.ntmbooks.com **or** books@ntm.org **or** 800.321.5375

Contents

Dedication

With thankfulness and praise to God, this series of books is dedicated to my parents who, by their words and godly example, taught me that the Written Word and the Living Word are the only solid and lasting foundations for this life and for eternity.

Foreword

Life is filled with storms. That's why you and I prefer to live and work in buildings that have solid foundations; we are more confident that they will endure severe forces.

Spiritual foundations are even more important because they build for eternity. We are daily bombarded with distractions and are tempted to wander from the simplicity that is in Jesus Christ. In order to stand firm in the faith, we need to be solidly anchored in God's Word.

Firm Foundations: Creation to Christ has been a great tool for evangelizing non-Christians and for instructing believers in the whole counsel of God. In this curriculum, each of the 48 lessons is interconnected, building on God's wonderful plan of redemption revealed chronologically in the Old and New Testaments. This systematic teaching of God's story produces spiritual strength in students as they gain an in-depth knowledge of Him.

As you use this tried-and-tested material, your investment in study, prayer and teaching will, by God's grace, reap eternal rewards and give stability in daily life.

Oli G. Jacobsen
Chairman, International Ministries
New Tribes Mission

Acknowledgments

Originally, I wrote the series entitled *Building on Firm Foundations* (BOFF) as source material for New Tribes missionaries who work cross-culturally with unreached people groups throughout the world. The lessons included many illustrations based on my own experiences as a missionary in the Philippines. Later, when some missionaries related to their sending churches and friends how God had wonderfully blessed the teaching of His Word based on the chronological approach laid out in BOFF, pastors and Bible teachers began adapting the lessons for their own congregations. It was against this background that it was decided to produce an adapted version of the earlier books of BOFF that would be better suited for teaching people living in modern societies.

Nancy Everson took up the challenge and offered to work with me on this project. Nancy assisted in adapting the original text and illustrations, developing visuals and adding cross-references. Never did we imagine that these lessons, entitled *Firm Foundations: Creation to Christ* (FFCC), would spread throughout the world and be translated into so many different languages.

Recently, a revised edition of the evangelistic phase of BOFF was published, so it was decided that FFCC should also be revised. I am deeply thankful to Ruth Brendle for her tireless efforts in seeing this project to completion. I also acknowledge the editing contributions made by Paul and Pam Rasmussen, suggestions from Don Pederson, illustrations drawn by Bill Pittenger, map and poster work by Doug Lotz, and the valuable input from my wife, Frances. I know that each one who has contributed in some way to these lessons joins with me in thanking the Lord for His grace and guidance throughout this endeavor. Our prayer is that the Bible lessons in these books will bring great glory to God and lead to the salvation of many.

L. Trevor McIlwain

PART 1

Why the Bible Should Be Taught Chronologically

1

The Master Builder's Plan

With a thunderous sound, the walls cracked and crumbled. Timbers splintered. The roof buckled, falling into pieces. Floor after floor crashed one upon another, crushing, trapping, killing the tenants. In a few moments, the high-rise apartments were reduced to rubble.

Investigation began to determine the cause of the disaster. Proof emerged, revealing that the builder had not followed proper specifications. Willing to gamble with the lives and the safety of human beings for the sake of money, he cut corners and economized.

The builder had disregarded the design specifications that the architect and engineers provided. He had followed his own way because it was easier and quicker and brought him greater profit.

The results? Sorrow! Destruction! Death!

It's just an example, but it speaks of what is happening all over the world when it comes to building the Church. Whether in evangelism or preaching and teaching of the Word of God, we often carelessly disregard our Master Builder's plans for building His Church. We are so engrossed in our own ideas, schemes and passions that we don't stop to consider if we are working according to God's divine directions or whether our work will pass His final scrutiny.

God's work of building His Church

God is the builder of His Church (Matthew 16:18). But He has chosen His earthly children to be partners together with Him (1 Corinthians 3:9).

The Christian's work in building the Church is similar to that of a building contractor. Just as a contractor is responsible to follow exactly the plans given to him by the architect, so we are responsible to follow God's plans for building His Church.

God is the true builder of all things. *"For every house is built by someone, but He who built all things is God"* (Hebrews 3:4).

God builds everything according to His eternal plans. He will not change. He will never accommodate man's ideas or modify His plans to go along with current trends. He will never permit any change in the specifications which He has laid down for all He has planned to do in what we call time. His work always has adequate foundations; He builds carefully, patiently and precisely. He refuses to take shortcuts in anything He does, and He never uses inferior materials or methods which are contrary to His holy and perfect nature.

The first account in Scripture of God's building work is when He created the heavens and the earth. *"By the word of the LORD the heavens were made, And all the host of them by the breath of His mouth .... For He spoke, and it was done; He commanded, and it stood fast"* (Psalm 33:6, 9). God was the Creator – builder of all things, seen and unseen. He created everything according to His perfect plan, and He declared that it was all good (Genesis 1:31).

Later in the Scriptures we have the account of God's command to Noah to build an ark. After commanding him to build the ark, God did not leave Noah to formulate his own plans. God told Noah exactly what must be done. Noah, God's faithful workman, did everything just as the Lord commanded him (Genesis 6:22).

When God chose to dwell with Israel, He commanded Moses to build the tabernacle. And how was Moses to build it? *"For He said, 'See that you make all things according to the pattern shown you on the mountain'"* (Hebrews 8:5). Every detail, from the silver sockets which were the foundations for the boards of the tabernacle to the outer coverings of badger skins, was to be made exactly according to the divine pattern shown to Moses on Mount Sinai. Moses faithfully followed these instructions. (Hebrews 3:2).

God's work of building the heavens and the earth was done by the power of His Word. Noah and Moses followed the words of God in all that they built. Likewise, God's present work of building His Church is also being accomplished through His mighty Word. *"For it is the God who commanded light to shine out of darkness, who has shone in our hearts to give the light of the knowledge of the glory of God in the face of Jesus Christ"* (2 Corinthians 4:6).

The building of the universe was the work of God alone. He did not use any angelic or human agent. But the great work of building the Church, like the work of building the ark and the tabernacle, has been committed to His children. *"We have this treasure in earthen vessels"* (2 Corinthians 4:7). *"We are ambassadors for Christ"* (2 Corinthians 5:20). *"You shall be witnesses to Me ... to the end of the earth"* (Acts 1:8). God has chosen to bring His Church to completion through the teaching of His Word by the members of the Church.

If the ark and the tabernacle had to be built exactly according to God's plan, should not the Church also be built according to His plan? Surely the Bride of Christ is of even greater importance than the ark or the tabernacle. The use for the ark came to an end, and the tabernacle was superseded by the temple, but the Church is to last for eternity. Therefore, *"If anyone defiles the temple of God, God will destroy him. For the temple of God is holy, which temple you are"* (1 Corinthians 3:17). Every man's work, in relationship to the building of the Church, is going to be tried by fire. It will all come under the scrutinizing gaze of the great Master Builder whose servants and co-laborers we are.

Whether we are seminary professors, pastors, missionaries, Bible class leaders, Sunday school teachers, youth workers, or concerned parents wishing to see our children taught the Word of God, *"We are God's fellow workers."* We must therefore be wise, taking careful note to make sure we are doing our work in the way He commanded (1 Corinthians 3:9-23).

Building as a wise master builder

Paul refers to himself as a wise master builder (1 Corinthians 3:10). He laid the foundations of the Gospel on which the Corinthians' faith and hope were built, and he warned the Bible teachers in Corinth to be careful how they built on those biblical foundations which he had laid (1 Corinthians 15:1-4).

When I began my ministry on the mission field, I realized that I had a similar responsibility to that which Paul had. I was responsible to lay the foundations of the Gospel and then build up

---
Teaching Principles Applicable Everywhere.

The chronological teaching principles presented in the *Firm Foundations* series grew out of my experiences on the mission field. You will notice as you read this book that many explanations and examples are from a missionary setting.

Please understand that the principles of chronological teaching are true regardless of where a person teaches. So, as you read this book, don't think, "Oh, that's just for missionaries." Following these biblical teaching principles is effective, whether teaching in a primitive jungle hut or in a metropolitan stained-glass church, or to a few people in a suburban home. Just as truth is truth no matter where you teach it, so also these biblical teaching principles are pertinent no matter where you use them.

---

the individual members of the Body of Christ in a remote island of the Philippines. I desired to be a wise master builder like Paul, but I wasn't sure how to be wise and careful as I built. I prayed for answers as the following questions gripped my mind and guided my search:

- By what standard did Paul judge his building methods and work and thus conclude that he was a wise master builder?

- How can all subsequent builders be sure that they are proceeding in the correct way and that their work will meet with divine approval?

- Has God only told us what to teach in His Word, or has He also shown us how to teach?

- Which is the clearest, most simple, and yet most comprehensive method of teaching the Word of God to prepare people for the Gospel, and to teach them God's way of salvation?

- How can we be sure that the foundations we lay, on which others are to rest their faith, will see them safely into Heaven and stand firm in the great day of testing?

- How should we teach in order to build up God's children and lead them into the knowledge of the whole counsel of God?

- What checklist should we use to determine if we are making headway, and whether the building is being brought to completion in accordance with the divine plan?

Years passed before I understood the answers to these questions. Why did it take so long? Because traditional Bible teaching methods influenced my thinking. I found the answers I needed when I finally looked to God's Word alone.

The effectiveness of biblical principles

After the Lord had shown me the biblical teaching principles that I present later in this book, He then opened opportunities for me to share these principles with others who were also searching. In 1980, I taught a seminar for missionaries in the Philippines. These biblical teaching principles excited and gripped the hearts of my co-workers who were struggling with problems identical to those I had faced in evangelism and in planting and guiding the development of churches to spiritual maturity. These missionaries returned to their work with fresh enthusiasm, for they now had clearer guidelines and precise goals for their teaching ministry.

Seminars were also held in Bolivia, Indonesia, Papua New Guinea, Senegal, Thailand and the USA. These initial seminars provided biblical guidelines for evangelism. The missionaries went back to their ministries and laid down firm foundations for saving faith in Christ by teaching a chronological overview of the Bible story, beginning in Genesis and concluding with the ascension of Christ.

The results were immediate and lasting. Many people from various tribal groups have come to a clear understanding of God's nature and character, their own sinfulness, helplessness and hopelessness, and Christ's all-sufficient saving work through His death, burial and resurrection. Their understanding of God's plan of salvation and the certainty of their faith far surpassed that of many others who had professed conversion previously. Furthermore, through chronological teaching, many of those sincere tribal people came to realize that they had misunderstood the missionaries' message when they were first taught. They are now trusting in a message which they clearly understand.

One of the first reports of great blessing came from Bob Kennell and George Walker. They had followed these scriptural methods when teaching the story of the Bible to the primitive, and previously unevangelized, Bisorio tribe in the Sepik region of Papua New Guinea. The Bisorio people responded to a message which they clearly understood from the Scriptures. Theirs is no blind faith, based merely on what the foreigner said. Instead, it is based on a clear understanding of the God of the Bible and the history of redemption.

Confusion about laying foundations

Christ and His Gospel are the only foundations which God has ordained as a basis for the faith of guilty sinners (1 Corinthians 3:11; 15:1-2). Nevertheless, there is great confusion, even among Christians, regarding these foundations and the correct way to establish them through preaching God's Word.

In the construction of any building, the foundations are the first part of the structure to be prepared. The majority of Gospel preaching, however, is usually done with very little foundational preparation. This lack has contributed to a multitude of false professions and the uncertainty of many new Christians about the foundations of their faith.

Another mistake Bible teachers tend to make is failing to teach the Bible consistently as one book, just as God has prepared it for us through progressive revelation. Teachers of the Word carefully devise and prepare outlines, but few stop to consider that the Bible has an inbuilt teaching outline, which, if followed, will give a clear, uncomplicated, comprehensive coverage of the entire Word of God.

Many teachers approach the Bible as if it were a treasure chest full of beautiful, precious gems. We assume that these jewels have not been given a definite pattern or design. We think that the responsibility is ours to arrange the jewels in some order which will enhance their beauty and cause them to be better appreciated. While recognizing the value of the Scriptures, many Bible teachers fail to see that there is a definite, divinely-given teaching outline which runs through the entire Word of God. We therefore proceed to arrange the Scriptures into what we consider to be comprehensive and lucid outlines. This is a basic mistake. Admittedly, good Bible teaching outlines are helpful; but too much time is spent developing methods and theories for Bible teaching, and insufficient time is given to simply teaching the Scriptures as they have been written.

The majority of Christian teaching emphasizes individual doctrines of the Bible rather than presenting the Bible as one complete, interdependent revelation of God. Heresies, misinterpretation, overemphasis of certain Scriptures, and denominationalism can, in most cases, be traced to this lack of chronological and panoramic Bible teaching.

After many years of listening to nonsequential, topical, doctrinal sermons, most of which are based on isolated texts, many church members still do not know the Bible as one book. Often-repeated verses and some doctrines may be known; but the Scriptures, according to their divinely given historical structure, are seldom understood.

This is equally true in Sunday school programs. Children are usually taught stories from the Bible out of chronological order, and large portions of God's Word are never taught to them at all. Even a faithful Sunday school pupil is unlikely to graduate with an overall knowledge of the Bible.

The approach when teaching the Scriptures in other lands to people without previous Bible knowledge has been similar. Few changes are made to the methods used in the homeland. Insufficient time is generally given to teach the Old Testament background and foundations for the Gospel. Syncretism of heathen and Christian beliefs is often the sad result. Many in foreign lands who have professed Christianity do not understand the Gospel, nor do they understand the Scriptures as one book.

Many missionaries are so eager to preach the Gospel that they feel it is an unnecessary waste of time to teach people too much of the historical portions of the Old Testament Scriptures. Nevertheless, these Old Testament historical sections form the basis for a clear understanding of the coming of Christ and the necessity of His

death, burial and resurrection. The Old Testament Scriptures, correctly taught, will prepare the heart of the believing sinner to receive the Gospel in true repentance and faith.

Objective and overview

The following chapters record my frustrations, my search, and also my joy at discovering divine teaching principles and guidelines in the Word of God. Additional volumes of *Firm Foundations: Creation to Christ* contain clear, simple, yet comprehensive lessons for the unsaved and the children of God which follow the flow of biblical history.

Through my own experiences, but more importantly, on the basis of the truth of God's Word, I will endeavor to show that the Scriptures were progressively revealed by God within the context and framework of history. Therefore, the best way to teach divine truth in any culture is God's way, within the chronological and historical framework of the Scriptures.

2

Check the Foundations

The Palawano tribe, living on the island of Palawan in the southwestern region of the Philippines, was downtrodden for centuries.

The proud, fierce Moros who lived on the smaller islands lying off the coast of Palawan oppressed these timid, fearful jungle people for many years. Numerous stories, now part of Palawano folklore, tell of the massacres and molestations of the Palawano tribal people by these marauding Muslim sea warriors.

Yet another oppression for the Palawanos came from Filipino settlers who migrated from other islands of the Philippines. They came seeking land for rice fields and coconut plantations, and for timber from the virgin forests for export. Many of these settlers took advantage of the native people of Palawan. They easily intimidated these unassuming, uneducated jungle people. Through fear of these aggressive settlers, many Palawanos left their ancestral lands and coconut plantations close to the sea for the less hospitable foothills and mountains of the island's interior.

Then came a time of even greater sadness and tragedy. Their island home was invaded by the Japanese. This was a fearful era in the Palawanos' history. Women were molested, and children were brutally murdered. Livestock was stolen and killed. Rice, their basic food, was often deliberately and maliciously scattered by the invaders as they knocked down the Palawanos' granaries. The suffering of these years surpassed all other segments of their inglorious history.

Then came an unexpected reprieve from their fear and degradation. The US liberation forces landed in Palawan. In all my years with the Palawano people, I heard only praise and admiration for these soldiers, never one word of reproach. While I was visiting in the homes of the tribal people, many of the older Palawano men asked me if I knew some particular officer by whom they had been befriended. They spoke of them with great affection. They obviously enjoyed remembering incidents when the "Amirikans" had warned the national Filipinos not to ill-treat the Americans' little Palawano brothers. The Palawanos saw it as a sad day when the US forces withdrew from Palawan, and their future became uncertain once again.

Years passed, and then, quite unexpectedly for the Palawanos, another American came to their part of the island. He was even more generous than all the other Americans they had known. Meanness and anger are frowned on in Palawano society. This missionary displayed love and kindness. Through his ministry and that of the missionaries who followed him, several thousand

Palawanos professed conversion to Christianity, but not understanding what it meant. They were baptized, and organized into indigenous churches.

When we arrived years later, we questioned the Palawanos as to why they had so readily submitted to baptism. One man answered, "We would have done anything for that first missionary. If he had asked us to cut our fingers off, we would have gladly done it for him."

The danger always exists that previously rejected and exploited people will respond to the Christian missionary's message, not because they see their real need as sinners and understand the Gospel, but because of genuine appreciation for the missionary and a longstanding desire to escape their difficult and degraded sociological conditions. This was the major reason for the people movement to Christianity, which took place almost immediately when the first New Tribes missionary preached to the Palawanos.

Confusion regarding the Gospel

Following this, more missionaries arrived to assist in the work. They faithfully taught the duties of believers to those who had professed conversion. Unknown to the missionaries, the majority of the Palawano church members interpreted the responsibilities of believers in the only way that they could as unsaved people. They thought the duties of the believer were the things they must do so they could continue to be "in God."

"In God" was the term the Palawanos usually used to describe their conversion to Christianity. They had come into God by their acceptance of Christ through faith, baptism, church attendance, singing, prayer, not stealing, and not committing adultery. The truly dedicated also thought that abstinence from alcohol, betel nut, and tobacco were necessary to guarantee their continued position "in God."

During their church meetings, they sometimes spoke of Christ and His death. More frequently, however, they testified of their faithfulness to the Lord by abstaining from sinful works and by church attendance. Obviously missing was praise to God for their salvation by Christ through His unmerited favor alone. Even though salvation by faith through grace alone had been taught, the majority had not clearly understood. They were trusting in a mixture of grace and works.

In spite of the emphasis on Christian living, many failed to live according to biblical standards. Divorce, remarriage and drunkenness were normal in the Palawanos' old way of life, and they continued to be major problems in all of the churches. The missionaries and the church elders were very concerned. They constantly exhorted the people to lay aside these old ways and follow the new way in Christ. The wayward church members would repent and function outwardly as Christians for a while; but often, they would fall back into their old ways until they were once again challenged and revived, starting the cycle all over again.

There were faithful individuals who were true believers among the Palawano people. However, the Palawano church as a whole was like a building that lacked the correct foundations. Large cracks appeared continually in the upper walls. The missionaries and church leaders spent their time running from church to church, trying to patch up the gaping holes. The problem was the people's basic foundational understanding of the Gospel.

Because most had turned to Christ for deliverance from their difficult lives and had never seen their own personal sinfulness and inability to please God, they had not realized that their only hope was to trust in God's provision for all sinners through the death, burial and resurrection of Christ. If they had trusted only in Him for God's acceptance, then their faith would have produced godliness and obedience to the commands of Scripture, not in order to obtain salvation, but as the fruit of true saving faith.

In 1965, my wife and I, along with our two children, began our work as missionaries with New Tribes Mission in the Philippines. We worked with the Palawano tribe over a period of 10 years. My responsibility was to see the elders and the churches brought to maturity through further instruction from the Scriptures.

Extensive hiking over the trails with the more zealous church elders was the only way I could reach and teach the more than 40 small churches scattered among the mountains and jungle. Through these visits to the Palawano churches, it soon became evident that the majority of the professing believers were confused and uncertain about the basic foundations of the Christian faith. They agreed with the necessity of Christ's death for man's salvation. However, most thought that Christ's death only secured a part of their salvation and that they were responsible to obtain the remainder of their salvation by obeying God.

The true spiritual condition of the people became apparent as I began to question them concerning their basis for salvation. I usually began by asking, "What must a person do to be saved?"

They were often reluctant to answer, but after some encouragement and direct questioning of individuals, they would begin to respond. Some answered, "Trust in God," and some said, "Believe on Christ."

To these answers, I replied, "What if a person truly believes and puts his faith in Christ as his Savior, but he does not attend church? Could he truly be saved?"

Many answered emphatically, "No!"

Others said, "Yes, if a person truly believes, he is saved, even if he does not attend church."

"But," I added, "what if that person is not baptized?"

Only a few thought that a person could be saved without baptism.

I then added what seemed, to many, to be the deciding point, "But what if that person who truly trusts in Christ were to get drunk or commit adultery? Could he really be saved?" Only a few in each congregation believed that such a person could be saved, and even they had grave doubts.

In addition to questioning, I found another method to be effective in determining what the Palawano church elders and Bible teachers believed. I would first teach them the truth and then contradict the truth by teaching error. In the Palawano culture, it is improper to contradict a teacher, because this could cause the teacher to lose face and become embarrassed. This, in turn, would cause the person who had contradicted the teacher to also be embarrassed. Even so, these church leaders needed to be taught to stand for God's Word, regardless of the cultural discomposure caused by confronting a teacher with the truth. False cults were increasing on the island, and these Palawano church leaders were faced with the endeavors of these false teachers to lead them and their congregations into error. I needed to be sure that these Bible teachers really understood the Gospel, that they were personally trusting only in Christ, and that they would be able to stand firm against false teachers. Of course, I only used this method after months of teaching these men. This method would not have been effective if used in the beginning of my association with the Palawano leadership. They would have verbally agreed with me in spite of what they actually believed in their hearts.

On one occasion, approximately one hundred Palawano elders and teachers had gathered for our monthly conference. I had taught for many hours from the Scriptures on salvation by grace through faith alone. Then, without warning or explanation, I began to teach faith plus works as the way of salvation. Then I paused abruptly and pointed to one of the men and asked him, "Is what I have just said correct? Is it true that sinners are saved, not only by faith, but by their good works?"

The tribal teacher hesitated and then finally answered, "No, it is wrong. We are saved by faith alone."

Feigning surprise, I continued to question him, "Do you mean to say you are telling me, the missionary, that I am wrong?"

Hesitatingly, he said, "Yes, you are wrong."

Still not giving them any clue to my real thoughts, I turned to another man and said, "He says that what I said was wrong. Do you agree or disagree?"

He answered, "What you said was wrong."

I then asked him, "How long have you been a Christian?" His answer indicated he was a much younger Christian than I.

"Oh!" I said, "I have been a Christian for many years. I have also been to Bible college. Do you still think I could be wrong?"

Again, he answered that I was wrong.

Even then, I did not show agreement or disagreement but turned to a third man and asked him what he thought. Much to my surprise, he said, "You are right!"

Thinking he had misunderstood, I repeated what I had said previously, stating that we are saved not only by faith but also by our good works.

Again, he said that my statements were correct.

I then asked him, according to my usual procedure, to give scriptural proof for his statement. To my even greater surprise, he turned to Ephesians 2:8-9. Hoping he would understand his mistake once he read these verses, I asked him to read them to all present. He did so and concluded by saying, "There it is. We are saved, not only by faith, but by our good works also."

Many of the men listening were now smiling, but I was looking to the Lord for wisdom in what to say to avoid embarrassing him.

I asked Perfecto, for that was his name, to read Ephesians 2:8-9 once again. He did but still maintained that these verses were teaching salvation through faith plus good works. I knew to simply tell him he was wrong would not establish the truth in his mind. It was important that he see for himself what these verses actually teach.

I said to Perfecto, "Those verses do not seem to be saying what you claim they do. Read them once again very slowly to yourself so you will understand what they really mean."

While we waited, Perfecto read the verses through slowly. Finally, he looked up at me with a look of great surprise and said, "No, I am wrong! We are not saved by faith and works, but by faith alone through God's grace."

The Palawano situation which I have described is not an isolated one. Multitudes throughout the world are members of evangelical churches but have no firm biblical foundations on which they build their hope for eternal life. Illustrations could be given from many areas of the world, including our own home churches, where confusion and syncretism have occurred through the sincere but unwise or careless ministry of Christian workers.

From South America, Dave Brown wrote in 1988 about the Guajibo churches in Colombia:

"The Guajibos have a long history of missionary activity. As early as 1650, the Jesuits made missionary trips into this territory which covers almost the entire eastern plains of Colombia. They were particularly interested in the Guajibo tribe, as it was the largest in this area (today numbering about 15,000). When the Jesuits entered the area, the Guajibos were still nomadic; but with the progress of time, they have now settled in small permanent villages. About 1958, news of a new religion called the 'Evangelical Way' began to trickle into this area. It immediately

attracted widespread attention; and before long, with the arrival of more information, many began to accept this new way of life. Today, almost 30 years later, this new influence from the outside world has made its mark on the Guajibo tribe. Many native-style, thatched-roof churches can be found throughout the region with religious meetings being held regularly.

"In each locality, a semi-annual evangelical conference is held. The first one I visited was attended by 700 Indians, some having traveled as far as a three days' walk. We were the first white missionaries to visit the area; and yet, here were 700 people gathered together to sing and preach to each other. Was there really any need for us as missionaries? Was this not a New Testament church in action? It was only the assurance that God had led us here that kept us.

"With the passing of time, serious problems have come to the surface in the Guajibo church. We are finding that they never really understood the message in the first place. Even those who seem keenest have hang-ups in the fundamentals of salvation. They quote catechismal answers to questions but do not understand the substitutionary work of Christ. 'Having a form of godliness, but denying the power thereof ...' (2 Timothy 3:5). And so, we have been forced to look back at the mistakes and failures of the past to try to determine where we are now, and to look to God for divine direction for the future."

How is it possible that people who attend church and have been taught the Gospel still do not understand that salvation is by the grace of God alone? Are we missing something in our preaching?

Shepherds should know their flock

While it is true that the Gospel can be understood and refused, there are other reasons why people can be part of evangelical churches but not be truly saved. One is because many pastors, youth leaders, missionaries, and Christian workers do not check the spiritual foundations of those whom they are teaching. Even when Christian workers do make the effort to find out what people are really understanding and trusting in for their salvation, few are willing to confront people with their true condition before God.

It was only through persistent questioning that I found out that some of the Palawano church elders and many members were ignorant of basic biblical truths and had misunderstood the way of salvation. The majority of the people had been trusting in a false message for more than 10 years, but the missionaries who had taught them were unaware of the misunderstanding in the people's minds. Certainly, we must be wise in questioning people; but many Christian teachers are so cautious not to offend that they rarely, if ever, find out the truth about their congregations.

Some Christian teachers think that knowing a person's spiritual condition is not their responsibility. They believe it is something which should be totally between a person and the Lord alone. But the Lord has given His people not only the responsibility to preach the Gospel to the unsaved but also the responsibility to be shepherds of the flock of God. How can we protect, strengthen, and feed them if we do not even know who are the sheep and who are the goats?

I freely admit, as one who is a Bible teacher and has served as a missionary and a pastor, that it is much more comfortable to teach from the pulpit than to face people on an individual basis in order to meet their real needs. Nevertheless, if we are to have an effective ministry and follow in the steps of the Chief Shepherd, we must have one-to-one contact with the flock.

The Gospels contain many accounts of our Lord Jesus' personal contacts and ministry with individuals. Three well-known encounters are Nicodemus (John 3:1-12), the Samaritan woman (John 4:1-26), and the rich young ruler (Matthew 19:16-22). In each of these encounters, Jesus made clear their true spiritual condition, and then He applied the correct spiritual remedy from the Word of God. The Apostle Paul's ministry also involved personal contact and exhortation (Acts 20:20, 31; Colossians 1:28).

Throughout the mission fields which I have visited, I have found a great reluctance on the part of many missionaries to seriously undertake this important task of knowing the true spiritual condition of each person under their care. Yet, it is unwise to instruct people in Christian living, merely hoping they have been born again. If we allow mere professors to act like God's children, even though they have no genuine faith in Christ, the result will be their everlasting damnation. This was the case in the Palawano churches. The great majority of professing Palawanos did not understand the Gospel. They had been instructed to live like Christians, but many were not children of God. Had they not been alerted to their grave danger, they would have gone on in this condition to an eternity without Christ.

One Sunday morning, after I had been teaching the Word of God in an evangelical church in Sydney, Australia, an elderly man said to me, "I am in deep trouble. I need to speak with you." Not knowing him personally, I did not understand what type of trouble he was referring to. The next day, I visited him in his home. As I sat talking with him, he said, "Your preaching has disturbed me. I have been a member of the church for 40 years, but I do not know the Savior." Later, I learned that, even though some fellow church members had wondered if he was saved, they had never questioned him. Most presumed he was a child of God. How sad if he had not finally faced up to his true condition before God!

An elderly Palawano man who had attended meetings for months came down to visit us from his little hut on the side of the hill. As we sat talking, I asked him, "Grandfather, what are you trusting in for your acceptance by God? What is your hope?"

He replied, "Grandchild, haven't I been coming to the meetings? When you pray, I close my eyes. I try to pray. I can't read, but I try to sing." And truly he did. He used to sit right at my feet and stare up into my face as I taught God's Word. He tried to do everything as I did it. But this old man had not understood the Gospel. He thought the things done in the meeting were a ceremony or ritual to please God in order to be accepted by Him.

I said to him, "Grandfather, if that is your hope, if you are trusting in what you are doing, then God will not accept you. When you die, you will go to Hell. God will not receive you because of these things." We continued to talk for some time about these matters before he returned home. Later, some of the people came and told me that Grandfather was angry and he was not going to come to any more meetings.

I thought, "That's good. That's a beginning. At least he now knows that attending meetings will not save him."

I began visiting Grandfather in order to teach the foundational truths of the Gospel to him personally. He listened attentively, and he did eventually begin once more to attend the meetings. But even when my wife and I moved from that area to live and teach in another place without any Gospel witness, he still had not made a clear profession of faith in Christ.

Sometime later, we returned to visit the church in the area where this old man lived. Stepping out of the Mission plane, I asked the tribal people who had run down to the airstrip to welcome us, "Is Grandfather still living?

They said, "Yes, he is. But he is blind and crippled."

Immediately, I made my way up the hill to his little old, rickety hut and sat down with him. He was pleased that I'd come. After visiting with him for a while, I said to him, "Grandfather, you are going to leave this world very soon. What is your hope? In what are you trusting for your acceptance by God?"

He answered, "Grandchild, it is like this. When I stand before God, I am not going to say to Him that I am not a sinner. God knows that I am."

I thought, "Well, praise the Lord! He has been taught that much of God."

He continued, "I am going to say this to God, 'God, You see Your Son there at Your right hand? He died for me!'" And then turning to me, he said, "Grandchild, won't God accept me because of Him?"

I answered, "Grandfather, He certainly will!"

Cultures and people differ. Not all cultures respond to questioning, regardless of our persistence. Nevertheless, it is important to find out what they understand and believe. If there is a more appropriate and cultural way to get this information than by questioning, it should be followed. But, regardless of our methods, we must ascertain the true spiritual condition of the people, for only then will we know the correct spiritual medicine they need from the Word of God.

What is the Gospel?

Another reason why some people in evangelical churches remain unsaved is the way in which the Gospel is presented. Many dedicated Christians present the Gospel in such a way that

unsaved, unprepared people do not understand that they deserve only God's judgment, that salvation is completely God's work, and that sinners are unable to contribute anything towards their own salvation.

Romans 1:3 tells us that the Gospel is God's good news *"concerning His Son Jesus Christ our Lord."* It is God's assurance *"that Christ died for our sins according to the Scriptures, and that He was buried, and that He rose again the third day according to the Scriptures"* (1 Corinthians 15:3-4).

The Gospel is first and foremost about Christ. It is the message of the finished, historical work of God in Christ. The Gospel is a work of the Godhead alone. Christ was *"smitten by God"* (Isaiah 53:4). *"It pleased the LORD to bruise Him; He has put Him to grief."* The Lord made *"His soul an offering for sin"* (Isaiah 53:10).

Many confuse the Gospel, God's work FOR us in Christ, with God's work IN us by the Holy Spirit. The Gospel is entirely objective. The Gospel is completely outside of ourselves. The Gospel is not about the change which needs to be made in us, and it does not take place within us. It was completed in Christ, quite apart from us, almost two thousand years ago. The Gospel is not dependent on man in any way. It is distorted when we turn people's eyes to what is to be accomplished in them. We were not and cannot be involved in any part of Christ's historical, finished, redemptive work. The sinner must be taught to look completely away from himself and trust only in Christ and His work of salvation.

The following is a portion of an article written by missionaries who are truly saved and very sincere, but the way they presented the Gospel is incorrect. In this article, they are giving an account of a conversation which they had with a tribal lady. They wrote, "Every Wednesday night, we visit Biaz' parents. We read a portion from Genesis and talk about it and ask questions. One night, Biaz said, 'I am so scared because the bad is in me, and I don't want God to throw me into the fire.'"

It is clear from this quote that Biaz was a soul prepared for the Gospel. There was an acknowledgement of personal sin and a fear of God's judgment.

But what was the answer of the missionaries? They told Biaz, "If you ask Jesus to throw the bad out of your liver and give you His Spirit, then you belong to Him and you don't need to be frightened anymore, and you will go to Him." Instead of the missionaries telling Biaz the historical, objective message of the Gospel as God's complete provision for her sin and God's coming judgment, they turned Biaz' attention to what needed to be accomplished within. What they taught Biaz was not the Gospel.

Unscriptural terminology

We distort and confuse the Gospel in people's understanding when we try to present the Gospel using terminology which turns people's attention to what they must DO rather than outward to what God has DONE on their behalf in Christ. We should use terminology which directs repentant sinners to trust in what has been done FOR them through Christ, rather than directing their attention to what must be done IN them.

Some common terminology is, "Accept Jesus into your heart." "Give your heart to Jesus." "Give your life to Jesus." "Open the door of your heart to the Lord." "Ask Jesus to wash away your sins." "Make your decision for Christ." "Ask Jesus to give you eternal life." "Ask God to save you." These commonly-used phrases confuse people's understanding of the Gospel.

As we prepare people for the Gospel, we must bring them to the point where they realize they can do nothing. But even when people do understand their inability to do anything, many evangelists, missionaries, and preachers tell enquirers things such as, "Now, you must give your heart to Jesus."

Having told them they are unable to do anything, they then tell them what they must do. What is the result? Confusion about the Gospel! People turn inward to their own experience, instead of outward to trust only in Christ's death, burial and resurrection on their behalf.

Methods and terminology used in evangelism all over the world have so distorted the Gospel that Christians need to be taught afresh the basic fundamentals of God's saving work in Christ, so their presentation of the Gospel will be according to the Word of God. Even though many people have been saved under present evangelistic methods, many others have not clearly understood the Gospel. The message they heard so emphasized man's part in conversion that God's perfect finished work and complete provision for helpless sinners in Christ was not understood and believed.

If people's attention is directed inward to their own doing, even those who are truly saved will often lack assurance of salvation. The question will constantly arise within their hearts, "Was I sincere enough? Did I do it correctly? Did I truly receive Christ? Did I really give my heart to Jesus?"

I have taught students in Bible College who were concerned and confused over these issues. One day, a student came to me deeply troubled. She talked with me about her conversion. She was concerned, "Did I do it in the right way? Was I really sincere? Did I really accept Jesus into my heart?" These questions plagued her. She had finally decided that, just in case she had not done it in the correct way, she would check with me to see what she should do.

At her conversion, she had realized she could do nothing to save herself. But the evangelist told her she must ask Jesus into her heart and give her life to Christ. From that time on, she was constantly concerned as to whether or not she had done all that she should have done. As I talked with her, I explained that it wasn't a matter of whether SHE had done it correctly or not, but whether the LORD JESUS CHRIST had done everything correctly on her behalf. Did He satisfy God? If so, was she trusting, not in her own doing, but in Christ's finished work on her behalf?

The Gospel is not man accepting Jesus as his Savior, but that God accepted the Lord Jesus as the perfect and only Savior two thousand years ago. The Gospel is not man giving his heart or his life to Jesus, but that Christ gave His life, His whole being, in the place of sinners. The Gospel is not man receiving Christ into his heart, but that God received the Lord Jesus into Heaven as the mediator of sinners. The Gospel is not Christ enthroned in the human heart, but that God enthroned the Lord Jesus at His right hand in Heaven.

Do we see the great distinction between these two messages? One is subjective and puts the emphasis on what man must do. The other is objective and puts the emphasis on what Christ has already done. The sinner is only to trust in what has already been done on his behalf. The Lord Jesus cried, *"It is finished."* He did it all. He took upon Himself the load of sin, the full responsibility for the sin of mankind. Because Christ paid the complete debt, God raised Him from the dead and accepted Him into Heaven. The resurrection was God's sign to all that He accepted the Lord Jesus Christ forever as the perfect Savior. God is satisfied. Is the convicted sinner? Will he rest the whole weight of his soul's salvation on Christ's acceptance by God as the perfect Savior? Will the sinner cease, once and for all, trying to do anything to save himself? Will he trust only in God's Son for salvation?

Some would call this type of Gospel presentation "Easy Believism." When they present the Gospel, they consider it is necessary to place before sinners the need to take up the cross and follow Jesus and the necessity of crowning Jesus Lord of their lives. Some preachers believe that, by insisting on this, they prevent people from making false professions. The answer to false professions, however, is not found in adding to the Gospel by requiring the sinner to promise to follow, obey, and suffer for Christ. There aren't any strings attached to the Gospel. The answer to true conversion lies in the correct preparation of the sinner's mind and heart for the Gospel. The Holy Spirit accomplishes this as the sinner hears and understands from the Scriptures that he is lost, helpless and hopeless, and stands condemned before God, who is his righteous, holy Creator and Judge.

Dependence on external, observable actions

This confusion regarding the presentation of the Gospel has another serious consequence. Multitudes, whose salvation is doubtful, assure themselves of their acceptance by God because, sometime in their life, they did what the preacher told them to do. They made their decision. They went forward and did what was required of them. Even though their lives have not been changed by the power of Christ and their way of life reveals an unconverted spirit, they still take refuge in what they did. They are trusting in what they did and not in what Christ has done. Multitudes of mere professors are resting their acceptance by God on their action of going forward or praying a prayer in response to the appeal.

Because much evangelistic preaching is subjective and experience-oriented, the attention of the hearers is placed on themselves and their personal response to the preaching. Christians excitedly report the salvation of little children, teenagers, and adults, taking it for granted that they have understood the Gospel and are truly converted, simply because they have displayed an outward decision for Christ.

In most evangelical circles, it is the norm to require people to publicly indicate their decision for Christ by raising their hand, standing, or walking to the front of the building, and praying a prayer of acceptance of Christ. The majority of Gospel preachers and Christians place so much emphasis on the invitation and people's outward response that many Christians are now convinced that it is an integral and vital part of the ministry of the Church. On one occasion, when a relative of mine clearly preached the Gospel but did not give a closing appeal, a Christian lady when leaving the meeting expressed her disapproval by the remark, "He didn't even give people the opportunity to be saved!" The danger is not that people are given the opportunity to publicly express their faith in Christ. The danger is the emphasis before and after the invitation which causes people to rest their salvation on their own personal actions in response to God, rather than on the actions of Christ which are declared in the Gospel.

When addressing this subject during a seminar with missionaries in the Philippines, I made the statement that I had never led any of the Palawano believers to the Lord, and I carefully explained what I meant. I had not asked the Palawanos to pray and to verbally accept Christ in my presence, nor did I tell them that they needed to pray a prayer of acceptance in order to be saved. I simply preached the Gospel and then exhorted the Palawanos to place their faith completely in Christ and the Gospel. Where, how, and what they actually did at the time of their conversion was not the important thing.

One missionary in the seminar strongly disagreed with my statement, "A person does not need to pray in order to be saved." When she objected, I replied, "Then I have led many people astray. I told the Palawanos that if they simply believed the Gospel and trusted in Christ, they would be saved. But I did not tell them that they must pray. According to what you are saying, I must now ask the Palawano believers if they prayed when they believed. If they did not, then I must tell them that unless they do, they will be lost."

Some people use Romans 10:9-10 to substantiate their claim that a person must make a verbal acceptance if he is to be saved. But this would then mean that mute people or those on their deathbeds who are beyond speaking would be unable to be saved. In addition, it would mean that unless a person was with someone else to whom he could confess with his mouth the Lord Jesus, he, too, would not be able to be born again. The first section of Mark 16:16 says, *"He who believes and is baptized will be saved."* Does this mean that baptism is necessary for someone to be saved? Of course not! The first part of Mark 16:16 must be interpreted in the light of the rest of the verse, *"but he who does not believe will be condemned."* All such Scriptures must be interpreted in the light of the unmistakable emphasis of the whole Bible – salvation in Christ is received through faith alone and is not dependent on any action of man.

On one occasion, during a conversation with another missionary, he told me how, many years earlier, he had come to assurance of salvation. His assurance came unexpectedly at the close of a meeting when the preacher asked everyone who was saved to raise his hand. Since, at that time, the man did not know if he was truly saved, he tried desperately to keep his hand down, but it was forced up by a power outside of himself. He related that, because of this experience, he never again doubted his salvation. Yet another Christian told me how she was assured of salvation through an unusual experience. When confronted by a wild, vicious bird, poised to attack her, she looked it in the eyes and said, "You can't touch me for I am a child of God." Because the bird did not peck her, she felt certain from that time that she was indeed in the family of God.

Experiences, regardless of their vivid and startling nature, should never be the grounds for believing that one is saved. The Word of God alone must be the foundation for assurance of salvation. John says of his Gospel, *"But these are written that you may believe that Jesus is the Christ, the Son of God, and that believing you may have life in His name"* (John 20:31). Each Christian is responsible to make certain that his preaching and evangelistic methods focus on Christ and His death, burial and resurrection as the only firm foundation for his hearers' assurance of salvation. Just as the physical eye does not behold itself but sees only the object on which it is focused, so true faith looks only to Christ. We should never accept any outward act of a professed convert as the basis for acceptance as a born-again person. The only scriptural basis for receiving a person's claim to salvation is his understanding and faith in the foundational truths of the Gospel.

In Palawan, a wizened, almost toothless old Palawano lady, who had been sitting for more than an hour on the front porch of our house, finally got around to her reason for visiting. Smiling, she said, "Grandchild, I am trusting in Jesus."

Even before she spoke, it was evident that she had something to tell me because she had patiently waited until all of our other visitors had gone home. Even though I had guessed that her news was related to her faith in Christ, it did not lessen my excitement and joy when she declared her dependence on the Savior. My natural reaction was to reach out and hug her, but Palawano decorum and culture, as well as a fear that such an action would seal her in a sincere but unfounded faith, restrained me. To immediately accept her testimony, without carefully questioning her, would not have been judicious. She might have been following the other members of her family who had already come in the preceding days to express their dependence on Christ and His redemptive work. For her own sake and for the fledgling church in that area of Palawan, I had to do whatever I could to ensure that her faith was resting on the foundations of Scripture which I had endeavored to lay down.

"Grandmother," I answered her, "It gives me great joy to hear that you are trusting in the Lord Jesus as your Savior. But why did you trust in Him? Why do you need the Lord Jesus?"

"I am a sinner," was her immediate answer.

"But Grandmother, why do you say that? You love your family. You are kind and a very hard worker."

"Yes, but I am a sinner before God," she insisted.

"But Grandmother, even though you are a sinner, why is it that you need the Lord Jesus? Why did you trust in Him? What has He done for you?"

"Ah, Grandchild, He was the One who died for me. He died for my sins."

Tears of joy filled my eyes as I replied, "Grandmother, I am so very glad to hear what you have said, for God's Word says that all those who trust only in the Lord Jesus as their Savior, believing that He died for them and then rose again, have all their sins forgiven by God and will never go to Hell. They have eternal life and will be received by God into Heaven."

How different was the testimony of this illiterate tribal woman compared to that of my wife's aunt, who went forward in response to an altar call at an evangelistic meeting in Australia. We were excited to think that this may be the first of Fran's relatives, outside of her immediate family, to be converted. So, while visiting with her, Fran began to question her regarding her profession. It soon became obvious that her aunt was taken up with her own personal feelings and experience rather than the historical accomplishments of Christ on her behalf. In an endeavor to determine her aunt's real grounds for assurance, Fran asked her, "Aunty, why did you go forward to the invitation of the preacher? Was it because you realized that you are a sinner?"

"Sinner? I'm not a sinner!" she exclaimed.

In spite of her lack of understanding of even the basic truths of Scripture, Christians had accepted her as having been saved simply because she had responded to the invitation.

Regardless of how careful we may be in questioning professing converts, there will always be those, as portrayed in the Parable of the Sower, who will appear to be Christians but will fall away after a time. Being fully aware of this danger is all the more reason why we should do everything we can to retain the purity, simplicity, and objectivity of the Gospel message, so that people will rest in the rightness of Christ's actions, and not their own.

3

People Unprepared for the Gospel

We have already used the biblical analogy of building to illustrate the work of preaching the Gospel. In addition, the Lord used the analogy of farming in His Word to teach us the correct procedures for doing His work. Therefore, I would like to tell you a parable about a farmer and his sons.

A man, leaving home for a period of time, left his sons with instructions to plant good seed throughout all of his fields. He provided them with the good seed and promised to return at harvest time.

Over the years, their father had written a book in which he recorded his experiences as a farmer. He explained how he had worked with each different type of soil. He recorded how he dealt with various weeds and conditions which hindered the growth of the good seed. Some of his accounts told of useless soil which produced only weeds and thorny bushes, and of other soil which, if properly prepared, had proven to be productive. His book indicated that all soil, even the best, needed lots of preparation and constant care if it was to yield a good harvest.

The sons were glad to obey their father; so in accordance with his command, they set off for the fields. They took with them the book and the good seed.

Arriving in the fields, they found large trees and an undergrowth of tangled vines and thorny weeds. Even the fields where their father had worked previously were now filled with weeds, and the ground was rocky and hard.

Feeling despondent, the sons took up their father's book and reread his last command. Yes, it was clear. They were to sow the good seed in every field. Therefore, as best they could, they set about to do what their father had commanded. One son cut away some of the undergrowth. After he had removed some of the weeds, he began to plant the good seed. Another son chopped down some of the trees, while another tore away the undergrowth with his bare hands before he put in the good seed. Each tackled the job with enthusiasm and vigor. They were passionate about farming but had little success.

With great devotion to their father's last command to sow the seed, they experimented with many different ideas and methods. Although their ideas seemed to bring results for a little while, eventually, the weeds choked most of the new plants or they died because of the hard rocky ground. Only a little of the seed actually took root and grew.

Meanwhile, their father's book, containing the account of his experiences and farming methods, was cherished but not applied to their own work.

Finally, in desperation, the sons took up their father's book and began to read how he had experienced problems which were exactly like their own. They carefully read his methods of preparation before he planted the good seed. Then, following his example, they chopped down the trees, dug up the weeds, ploughed, fertilized, and watered the ground. Once the ground was broken up and well-prepared, they planted the good seed.

As a result of following their father's recorded methods and principles, more and more seed took root and flourished.

Unprepared ground

In Jeremiah 4:3, the Lord says, *"Break up your fallow ground, and do not sow among thorns."*

This verse teaches a spiritual principle which is emphasized continually throughout the Scriptures. It also highlights one of the greatest failures in most evangelism. The majority of evangelists, preachers, and teachers at home and on the mission field do not spend sufficient time preparing the minds and hearts of people before they offer the Gospel to them. The Gospel seed is usually sown into hard, unplowed, poorly prepared, thorny ground. In many cases, the results are professions which last only for a short time. There is little permanent growth and fruit.

In the Parable of the Sower in Matthew 13:3-8, some seed fell on the wayside, some on shallow ground, and some among the thorns. This seed was soon taken away, withered or choked. Some people believe this parable is teaching us that it is our responsibility to sow the seed of the Gospel, regardless of the condition of the hearts of our hearers. It is true that there will always be the types of people illustrated by the Parable of the Sower. Even some who claimed to believe and follow our Lord Jesus were false professors. But what is Jesus really teaching through this parable?

Was Jesus teaching that we should sow the seed on unprepared and rocky soil? Did the farmer plan to sow seed on the wayside? Was it his intention to sow seed among the thorns? Did he think he would receive a harvest from seed sown on shallow, rocky soil? Of course not! This farmer had prepared the ground in order to plant it with good seed. His purpose was to plant the seed only in the ground which he had prepared. He did not intentionally throw good seed onto unprepared ground. However, as he sowed the seed on prepared ground, some of it fell on unprepared soil. None of the seed which fell on unprepared soil yielded a harvest. The main point Jesus is teaching through the Parable of the Sower is that good seed grows well and bears fruit only in prepared soil.

The human heart is not naturally good soil for Gospel seed. The history of man recorded in the Scriptures makes it clear that no descendant of Adam is naturally inclined towards God or His way of salvation. *"There is none who understands; there is none who seeks after God"* (Romans 3:11). *"And the way of peace they have not known. There is no fear of God before their eyes"* (Romans 3:17-18). *"The carnal mind is enmity against God; for it is not subject to the law of God, nor indeed can be"* (Romans 8:7). These verses clearly teach that the unsaved person's heart and attitude is hostile towards God. The unsaved person doesn't see any reason why he should submit himself to what God says. Furthermore, he is unable, in his own strength, to do what God requires of him.

The natural person may follow false religions and serve man-made gods or even what he believes to be the true and living God. Some will gladly accept a gospel which sounds like the true Gospel of Christ. According to the Scriptures, however, no person seeks the true and living God or can come to Christ by faith unless God first seeks him out by His Spirit through His Word (John 6:44-45).

Felt needs

In recent years, in many missionary circles, an unscriptural emphasis has been placed on felt needs as the basis for the presentation of the Gospel. Some teach emphatically that, if the Gospel is to be acceptable, meaningful, and relevant to our hearers, we must first discover and understand their felt needs and then offer the Gospel as God's answer to these felt needs.

Those who stress felt needs as the key for understanding and accepting the Gospel are confusing the results and blessings of the Gospel with the Gospel itself. Remember, the Gospel is the message of the finished, historical, redemptive work of God in Christ. The Gospel was not given by God to satisfy the natural desires of any human being, regardless of his culture. Jesus Christ's prime mission in the world was not to make people happy, peaceful, secure, or even to provide them with a sense of belonging and feeling loved. These basic human desires are also important to God, but they are not the issues in the presentation of the Gospel. They are the fruit of the Gospel and should be experienced in the lives of those who believe the Gospel. The Gospel which we preach, however, is not sent by God as good news to those whose basic quest is to be happy, peaceful, secure, healthy, or who simply want to go to Heaven. These are natural desires and may also be the fruit of the evil, self-centered nature of man. Even the most ardent atheist or depraved criminal usually desires these things.

Offering the Gospel on the basis of natural desires or culturally felt needs places man and his desires at the center of our message. Thus, man and his happiness are enthroned; and God's objective through the Gospel, when presented this way, is to satisfy man's needs, whatever man feels them to be. This is not scriptural. God does not exist for man. Man exists for God. *"You are worthy, O Lord, to receive glory and honor and power; for You created all things, and by Your will they exist and were created"* (Revelation 4:11).

Did Jesus come into this world to meet felt needs? No! He came to settle the problem of sin. John wrote, *"And we have seen and testify that the Father has sent the Son as Savior of the world"* (1 John 4:14). The angel told Joseph, *"You shall call His name JESUS, for He will save His people from their sins"* (Matthew 1:21). *"The Son of Man has come to seek and to save that which was lost"* (Luke 19:10). The mission of our Lord was to deal, first and foremost, with the matter of man's separation from God because of sin. Sin is an affront to God and His position as Sovereign Creator and Ruler. This is why the Son said to His Father, *"Behold, I have come to do Your will, O God"* (Hebrews 10:9). Jesus fulfilled His mission by suffering the righteous judgment of a holy God.

Jesus did not try to meet the people of His day on the basis of their understanding of their needs. In Jesus' day, the natural desire of the average Jew was for a king or political figure who would deliver Israel from the oppression of their enemies. After Jesus had fed the five thousand, He knew that the people were going to try to take Him by force and make Him their king, so *"He departed again to the mountain by Himself alone"* (John 6:15). The following day, the crowds looked for Jesus because they wanted to be fed. Jesus, however, did not respond to them on the basis of these felt needs. Instead, He told them their real needs as God saw them. He offended so many by His message that John tells us, *"From that time many of His disciples went back and walked with Him no more"* (John 6:66). Most Jews rejected Jesus' assessment of their needs. They refused to acknowledge their great need of a Savior to release them from sin which was controlling their lives and leading them to eternal separation from God.

Paul records that the Gentile world was more interested in human wisdom and philosophy than in salvation from the depravity and condemnation of its sins. To both the Jew and Gentile, unprepared by God, the preaching of the Cross was irrelevant and foolish. Yet Paul did not accommodate the Gentiles' quest for wisdom or the Jews' desire for signs and miracles. Paul preached the Gospel, God's power which saves believing sinners. He said, *"but we preach Christ crucified, to the Jews a stumbling block and to the Greeks foolishness"* (1 Corinthians 1:23). Paul reminded the Corinthian believers, *"And I, brethren, when I came to you, did not come with excellence of speech or of wisdom....my speech and my preaching were not with persuasive words of human wisdom"* (1 Corinthians 2:1, 4). Paul knew the felt needs of the people in wicked Corinth were not sound foundations for the Gospel. Paul knew that *"the natural man does not receive the things of the Spirit of God, for they are foolishness to him; nor can he know them, because they are spiritually discerned"* (1 Corinthians 2:14).

The Holy Spirit came into the world to convince the world of sin, righteousness, and judgment (John 16:8). Jesus came to call sinners to repentance (Matthew 9:13). God *"commands all men everywhere to repent"* (Acts 17:30). The biblical basis for the Gospel is a sense of our sinfulness before God and the recognition that only God's mercy and grace can provide us with forgiveness of our sins. No culture naturally recognizes this spiritual need.

When the majority of Palawanos first professed conversion, they had responded because of culturally felt needs and not because of spiritual needs taught by the Holy Spirit. They embraced Christianity for the wrong reasons. Being animists, they were convinced that their well-being, physically and materially, was dependent on their ability to placate and manipulate the spirits to keep the spirits happy and contented. Many who professed conversion took a similar attitude towards God. They interpreted God and what He wanted from them according to their own cultural worldview. They tried to please God and gain His acceptance by being baptized, reading the Scriptures, and meeting together to sing and pray. They tried to keep what they understood to be the Christian rules so they would experience God's blessings on their lives.

Previously, when they believed the spirits healed them, they offered a thanksgiving feast. They believed this was necessary so the spirits would be satisfied and not do them any further harm. Later, when they attributed their healing to God, many believed it was obligatory to go to church and give a thanksgiving testimony telling all that had taken place during their sickness and healing. Such testimonies usually concluded with the words, "Therefore, God is really true." Because they syncretized their old beliefs about the spirit world with their limited understanding of God and Christianity, they thought that the Lord's healing was the greatest proof that God was real, just as in previous years they had trusted in the spirits and their power to heal. God's power and goodness in healing them and meeting their physical needs were extremely important to them and the basic reason for their faith in Him. But when it appeared that God failed to answer their prayers, many turned back to the spirits and the witch doctors to meet their felt needs. Their Christianity did not last because it was based on felt needs instead of spiritual needs revealed by God.

Having said this, I am not implying that the Lord does not care about people's feelings or their needs. He does, but He knows that a person's needs cannot be met unless he first allows God to meet his primary and greatest need – to be reconciled to God. Because God cares about people's feelings and hurts, we should also. Even so, if we really want to be ministers of good to them, we must prepare sinners to see their real needs from God's perspective.

Ignorance and misunderstanding

The heart must be prepared by God for the reception of the Gospel. Man's evil heart, with its natural, self-centered desires, is not fertile soil for the good seed of the Gospel. Furthermore, the preaching of the message of salvation through Christ will not bear fruit where people's minds remain in darkness, unenlightened to spiritual realities. Saving faith rests on the comprehended truth of God.

In the book, *Through the Looking Glass* by Lewis Carroll, the Queen tells Alice:

'Now I'll give you something to believe. I'm just one hundred and one, five months, and a day.'

'I can't believe that!' said Alice.

'Can't you?' the Queen said in a pitying tone. 'Try again: draw a long breath, and shut your eyes.'

Alice laughed. 'There's no use trying,' she said: 'One can't believe impossible things.'

'I dare say you haven't had much practice,' said the Queen. 'When I was your age, I always did it for half an hour a day. Why, sometimes I've believed as many as six impossible things before breakfast.'

One eminent Bible teacher quoted this dialogue, pointing out that unregenerate people are mistakenly convinced that the meaning of faith is, "Take a long breath; close your eyes to facts, to reality, and believe."

God always works within the realm of the mind. Truth is presented to the intellect to be heard, understood, and believed. It is surprising that, in spite of the emphasis of the Scriptures on the need for truth to be understood, many Christians do not see it as a basic necessity for true saving faith.

The main reason for the confusion among the Palawano people was their ignorance of the Gospel as well as their ignorance of the truths which are given by God as the only preparation for the Gospel.

One day I was hiking with a missionary who felt I expected the tribal people to understand too much biblical truth before I would accept them as true children of God. We were discussing the confusion in the minds of the Palawanos regarding the way of salvation.

He made the statement, "When I was saved, I didn't know anything."

I replied, "If you didn't know anything, you didn't get saved. Tell me, what did you do when you got saved?"

"I trusted in Christ," he answered.

"But why did you trust in Christ and not Mohammed or Buddha?"

"I trusted in Christ because I knew that He died for me."

I questioned further, "But why did you need someone to die for you?"

"I knew I was a sinner going to Hell," he answered.

"Well, it appears you did know something after all," was my response.

In the Parable of the Sower, the Lord Jesus said, *"When anyone hears the word of the kingdom, and does not understand it, then the wicked one comes and snatches away what was sown in his heart. This is he who received seed by the wayside"* (Matthew 13:19).

When Philip met the Ethiopian eunuch and heard him reading from the Prophet Isaiah, Philip asked, *"Do you understand what you are reading?"* (Acts 8:30). Philip recognized that this man could never exercise true saving faith unless he first understood what the Word of God teaches about salvation.

When a person is saved, he may not know some scriptural truths, but he will know certain facts. He will know that God is the righteous, holy

Judge of all. He will also know that he is a sinner before God and that he can do nothing to save himself. Furthermore, he will know that Christ died to pay the complete price for the forgiveness of his sins and that Christ rose from the dead. This is the Gospel which the Apostle Paul preached. *"I declare to you the gospel which I preached to you, which also you received and in which you stand, by which also you are saved, if you hold fast that word which I preached to you – unless you believed in vain"* (1 Corinthians 15:1-2). This is the Gospel which must be heard, understood and believed if a person is to enter into God's salvation.

One day two Palawano men who were teachers in their local church sent a message to me, asking me to come and baptize them. I was not aware that these men had not been baptized, as almost everyone had been baptized many years earlier when they first professed to believe.

A Filipino trainee missionary accompanied me to their village. We also sent a message to the leading elders from another, more established church, requesting they meet us in the village where these two men lived. My companion and I agreed not to raise the question of baptism but to teach on salvation by grace through faith alone.

We taught for two days both publicly and privately, focusing our teaching on the sinful, helpless condition of man, the Gospel, and justification by faith alone. The two men who had requested baptism were in the public meetings and also the group discussions. We purposely did not raise the matter of their desire to be baptized because we were not convinced they really were clear on salvation by grace alone. If through the teaching they realized they were unsaved, we wanted them to be able to decide not to be baptized without any embarrassment. If they raised the matter of their baptism, we would question them, in order to determine what they were trusting in for their salvation.

At the close of the final meeting, the men asked publicly if they could be baptized. Knowing the misunderstanding which most of the Palawanos had about baptism, I asked the men why they wished to be baptized.

Regardless of all the teaching we had given on salvation apart from works, one of them answered, "So that I will really know God."

I asked him to open his New Testament to John 14:6. "Ontoy," I asked, "Does your Bible say, 'The river is the way, the truth, and the life. No man comes to the Father but by baptism?'"

He answered, "No."

I said, "Ontoy, if you die and you are trusting in baptism to get you to God, you will go to Hell. God will not accept you."

After some more teaching, we returned home. Several months later, Ontoy hiked from his village to our home for some medicine. As he stepped onto our verandah, I took his hand and, looking into his face, I asked, "Ontoy, how is it with you? Do you now know the truth?"

Ontoy replied, "Yes, I know the Lord!"

He continued by saying, "Brother, when you told me that I would go to Hell if I was trusting in baptism, it was like a knife in my liver. I love you, and it hurt when you spoke to me like that. But I want to thank you for telling me the truth. I would have died and gone to Hell. Now I am trusting only in Christ."

Both of those men came to a clear understanding of the Gospel and trusted in the Lord Jesus as Savior. Their testimonies were very clear when, at a later date, some of the Palawano church elders baptized them.

Faith is not some mystical feeling. It is not mere hoping or blind chance. Faith is not intellectual suicide. It is not contrary to reason. Saving faith is based on objective, historical, biblical facts. Saving faith is well-grounded. True faith rests on the sure Word of God. The Gospel therefore must be understood if it is to be believed to the saving of the soul. If the sinner is to exercise true saving faith, there must be enlightenment by the Holy Spirit through the Word of God.

The salvation which God offers sinners rests on a simple understanding and faith in the Word of God concerning the death, burial and resurrection of the Lord Jesus. God, in the person of Christ, stepped into history and acted on our behalf. He lived, died as our substitute, and rose again. A person exercises faith when he looks away from all self-effort to the saving history of Christ and depends only on Him and His work of salvation on the sinner's behalf.

4

Foundations for the Gospel

The Gospel is God's good news about His Son. But to whom does God offer this good news? Whom does God call to eat the bread of life? To whom does He offer the water of life?

It is clear from God's Word that He offers good news to those who know they are spiritually poor. He offers bread to the hungry, water to the thirsty, rest to the weary, and life to the dead. God's good news is meant for all, but the person unprepared by God will never accept God's Gospel of grace. God knows that, and He tells us not to throw the pearl of the Gospel before swine, that is, to those who sense no need to be saved from their sins and have no appreciation of God's mercy (Matthew 7:6).

In the book of Matthew, we read, *"Now it happened, as Jesus sat at the table in the house, that behold, many tax collectors and sinners came and sat down with Him and His disciples. And when the Pharisees saw it, they said to His disciples, 'Why does your Teacher eat with tax collectors and sinners?' When Jesus heard that, He said to them, 'Those who are well have no need of a physician, but those who are sick. But go and learn what this means: "I desire mercy and not sacrifice." For I did not come to call the righteous, but sinners, to repentance.'"* (Matthew 9:10-13). Because the Pharisees were self-righteous, Jesus did not invite them to come to Him. He told them

to first "go and learn." What were they to learn? They needed to learn that they were unable to offer God anything which could satisfy His holy and righteous demands and, therefore, they were in need of the mercy of the Lord. It is only to those who are heavily laden with the realization of their sinfulness before God that Jesus gives His gracious invitation, *"Come to Me, all you who labor and are heavy laden, and I will give you rest"* (Matthew 11:28).

God sent John the Baptist to do this necessary work of preparing Israel to receive their Messiah and His Gospel (Matthew 3:1-12). But the self-righteous religious leaders refused to accept John's message of condemnation. They remained obstinate, unwilling to consider the truth. In the book of Luke, we read, *"And when all the people heard Him, even the tax collectors justified God, having been baptized with the baptism of John. But the Pharisees and lawyers rejected the will of God for themselves, not having been baptized by him"* (Luke 7:29-30).

Jesus also said to the people of His day, *"For judgment I have come into this world, that those who do not see may see, and that those who see may be made blind"* (John 9:39). Those who realized they were spiritually blind would be given spiritual understanding through the truth which

Jesus spoke, but those who, like the Pharisees, refused to acknowledge their ignorance would remain forever in spiritual darkness. When Jesus said this, *"some of the Pharisees who were with Him heard these words, and said to Him, 'Are we blind also?' Jesus said to them, 'If you were blind, you would have no sin; but now you say, "We see." Therefore your sin remains.'"* (John 9:40-41). The proud Pharisees believed they were already enlightened and that they understood perfectly the will of God. They felt no need to receive spiritual sight, for in their own estimation they could already see quite well. They claimed to be guides of the blind (Romans 2:17-20). Why, they felt, should they allow this man to teach them? Because they didn't see their great need, and instead claimed they already had spiritual sight, they were left to perish in their blindness. They never understood the grace of God available through the Gospel.

When addressing the same hardened Jewish leaders after Christ's resurrection and ascension, Stephen said, *"You stiff-necked and uncircumcised in heart and ears! You always resist the Holy Spirit; as your fathers did, so do you"* (Acts 7:51).

Nicodemus came seeking Jesus, but Jesus did not immediately tell Nicodemus the good news of the Gospel. Instead, Jesus told him that he needed to be born again (John 3:1-7). Teaching about the necessity of the new birth is not the Gospel. The Gospel is God's good news that Christ died for sinners, He was buried, but after three days God raised Him from the dead (1 Corinthians 15:1-4).

Like his fellow Pharisees, Nicodemus was depending largely on his birth as a son of Abraham for his acceptance by God. Knowing this, Jesus first faced Nicodemus with the impossibility of his entering God's kingdom by virtue of his Jewish birth or his own goodness. Jesus then told Nicodemus the Gospel (John 3:14-16). One can only appreciate Christ's work on his behalf if he has first realized the impossibility of saving himself.

While on a visit back to Palawan, I was asked to teach a seminar for some of our missionaries on the chronological approach to evangelism and church planting. During one of our sessions, I emphasized that, if a person's mind is filled with his own self-righteousness, he will not see any need or feel any hunger for the Gospel.

A young Palawano man who was attending the seminar could not understand this particular point. One morning, this young man ate breakfast with us, part of which was scrambled eggs. After we had finished eating, I turned to him and asked if he was hungry and if he would like something to eat. He assured me he didn't feel like eating anything. Nevertheless, I continued to insist. I told him that my wife, Fran, would be only too glad to get him something to eat.

Realizing what I was aiming at, Fran also assured him that it wouldn't be any problem for her to cook some scrambled eggs. Again, he thanked us but declined our offer. Feigning sincerity and concern, I repeated the offer and tried to get him to let Fran cook some scrambled eggs for him.

By this time, he thought I was crazy. Emphatically, he said, "But I am not hungry."

"That's right," I answered, "You ate a good breakfast. You are not hungry. You have no appetite for food."

"Oh! Now I see!" he exclaimed.

As it is in the natural realm, so it is in the spiritual. As long as people are filled with their own self-righteousness, it is useless to try to force the Gospel on them. The Gospel is for the hungry, for the thirsty, and for the weary. It is for those broken before God through a realization of their own sinfulness.

How is a person brought to this realization? How is the heart of man prepared for the Gospel? The Holy Spirit uses the Word of God to prepare the mind and heart of a person for the Gospel.

But what particular part or message from God's Word accomplishes this preparatory work?

The knowledge of God

Years after missionary work had begun in a highland tribe in Papua New Guinea, some of the people announced that they were not going to tithe anymore. Why? Because they had decided that they had repaid God enough for giving Jesus to die for their sins.

The judicial system of this group was based on a monetary pay-back arrangement, so it is easy to see why they thought they had to recompense God for giving Jesus to die for their sins. But why did they think it was possible to pay God back for the gift of His Son? What didn't they understand?

These people obviously had failed to comprehend the nature and character of God as revealed in the Old Testament, and finally in the Gospel. They thought God was like the spirits and human beings. Because they demanded pay-back, they thought God did also. To have told them that salvation is a gift would not be sufficient. They needed to see, through the Scriptures, the true nature and character of God. If they were to see God as He really is, they would have also seen themselves as helpless and hopeless sinners. In the light of God's majesty and their own depravity, they would have understood the futility of every endeavor to pay God back.

Furthermore, they had failed to comprehend the consequences of sin. Through the teaching of the Old Testament, beginning with God's warning to Adam regarding the tree of the knowledge of good and evil, *"in the day that you eat of it you shall surely die"* (Genesis 2:17), they should have realized that death, eternal separation from God, is God's just judgment on sinners. This emphasis on death as the only payment for sin continues through the Old Testament historical accounts of God's judgment on sinners, and ends with the New Testament account of Christ's death as the only satisfactory payment for sin. If the tribal people had understood the Old Testament emphasis on death, they would have also recognized that only the death of Christ could pay for sin and satisfy God who is holy and righteous.

Another example is the Aziana tribe in Papua New Guinea. These people were sun worshipers. Missionaries claiming to preach Christianity preceded New Tribes missionaries into this area. But in spite of being missionized, the Aziana people had no clear understanding of the God of the Bible. They thought He must be similar to their sun-god.

In their ceremonial worship of the sun, they killed a pig, cooked a mixture of its liver and blood in a piece of bamboo and, as the sun set, they gathered together to worship and appease the sun. The priest first ate of the cooked blood and liver, after which all present partook. The priest also spat some of the mixture at the sun to blind it, so their sins would not be seen and avenged. They believed this would appease the sun, a malicious and malevolent god, and make their souls invisible to it.

When the first missionaries to the Aziana people taught them to commemorate the Lord's Supper, the people gave it the same name as this feast to the sun. They believed that by partaking of the Lord's Supper they were appeasing God and blinding Him to their sins. But these people would never have misinterpreted the Lord's Supper in this way if they had been taught and understood who and what God is. They would have realized that God is not malicious in His intents, that He cannot be appeased like their heathen deities, and that He, the omniscient, immutable God, can never be blinded to man's sinfulness. These people were not prepared for the Gospel because they did not have an understanding of the holiness and righteousness of God. Because they had never been exposed to the knowledge of God, they did not see themselves as incapable of doing anything which would please God.

Job, David, and Solomon all stated the truth: True wisdom begins with a solemn appreciation of who and what God is. *"The fear of the LORD is the beginning of wisdom"* (Psalm 111:10). Only those whose senses have been tuned to know and accept something of God's nature, character and sovereign position are prepared for the Gospel.

If God is not truly God, as revealed foundationally in the Old Testament, and finally in the New Testament through Jesus Christ, then there is no need for the Gospel. Only those who are enlightened through this revelation of God as a righteous and holy God, who hates and punishes sin, will see their need for the Gospel.

Because God is man's sovereign Maker, He is also his Owner, Lawgiver and Judge. If this is not true, then man is a free agent and cannot be called to give an account of himself to God. Man's great desire to be free to live only for himself and the satisfaction of his selfish, depraved, insatiable lusts has caused him to hate, flee from and endeavor to destroy the knowledge of God, his rightful Master.

But even when people understand that God is their Owner, Lawgiver and Judge, if God is not also seen as holy and righteous, then there is no need for the Gospel. God is not someone who will tolerate, overlook or forgive sin without full retribution. God is perfectly righteous. His own holy character is the standard for goodness; therefore, anything which does not agree with, or is contrary to what He is, is sin. Anything less than what God is, is totally unacceptable to Him.

God's holiness and righteousness are clearly revealed in history by His consistent hatred and judgment of the least departure from His holy standard. God will not overlook sin. All sin must be paid for. *"The soul who sins shall die"* (Ezekiel 18:4). Because God is righteous, He will never lower His standard of holiness or accept anything less than the full, righteous payment for sin.

As long as people are ignorant of God's holiness and righteousness, they will never understand their desperate need for the grace of God in Christ. They may give lip service to the Gospel, speak about Christ, attend church, sing hymns, read the Bible, pray, and even seek to serve Christ, but they will still be unsaved. Man is by nature self-righteous and will never let go of his pride and self-confidence until he realizes God's infinite holiness and righteousness. The unsaved religionist does not understand God's holiness and righteousness, for he is constantly trying, by his own good works and religious activities, to place God in a position where God will feel obligated to accept and bless him.

This knowledge of God, which man naturally hates and seeks to escape, is nevertheless man's greatest need. Apart from a knowledge of God, man will never truly repent, believe and be saved. A revelation of God's nature and character is prerequisite to the realization of one's own unrighteousness and abject helplessness to escape the just judgment of God. It was only after Job received clear awareness of God's character that he said, *"I have heard of You by the hearing of the ear, but now my eye sees You. Therefore I abhor myself, and repent in dust and ashes"* (Job 42:5-6).

Isaiah, when called to be God's prophet, needed a realistic assessment of himself and his people. Only then could he speak in true humility against the sinfulness of the nation. How then did the Lord show Isaiah his true self and the iniquity of his nation? Isaiah was given a vision of the Lord in all His sublime glory, sovereignty and holiness. The immediate effect on Isaiah was to cry, *"Woe is me, for I am undone! Because I am a man of unclean lips, and I dwell in the midst of a people of unclean lips; For my eyes have seen the King, the LORD of hosts"* (Isaiah 6:5).

All people, regardless of their religious or cultural background, must be led down this road of the revelation of God. Only an understanding of who God is will produce true self-knowledge, genuine repentance and saving faith.

Jesus said, *"No one can come to Me unless the Father who sent Me draws him; and I will raise him up at the last day. It is written in the prophets, 'And they shall all be taught by God.' Therefore everyone who has heard and learned from the Father comes to Me"* (John 6:44-45). Every person who ever comes to Christ for salvation comes because he has been taught, through the revelation of God's character as revealed in the historical sections of the Scriptures, that God is holy and righteous and will not overlook sin.

The Law

The Law is yet another means which God uses to prepare the sinner for the Gospel and the realization that, without Christ, he will perish.

By the fall of man and through subsequent history, man has been made aware of his sinfulness through revelations of God's holy character and will. Why then was the Law given? *"The law entered that the offense might abound"* (Romans 5:20). The Law was brought in to classify and clearly define sin. God gave the Law to fully expose man's sinfulness and, thus, to prepare the human heart for the Gospel. *"The law was our tutor to bring us to Christ, that we might be justified by faith"* (Galatians 3:24). God gave the Law to Israel, not to save them, but to show them the impossibility of salvation by human goodness. *"By the deeds of the law no flesh will be justified in His sight, for by the law is the knowledge of sin"* (Romans 3:20). *"The law brings about wrath"* (Romans 4:15). The Law reveals God's wrath against sin and shows that man can only approach God if the complete, righteous demands of His Law are paid in full.

Jesus told the self-righteous Pharisees to go and learn that sinners are saved by God's mercy and not by their own sacrifices to God (Matthew 9:13). How were the Pharisees to learn this? Who or what was God's ordained teacher? How could they see their true condition before God as helpless sinners needing a Savior? It was through a correct understanding of the Law!

The Jews had the written Law of God, but the scribes and Pharisees had given it such a carnal interpretation that it did not convict them of their inner heart attitudes. They did not understand the Law as God intended it to be understood. If they had, they would have realized the impossibility of anyone ever obeying it perfectly; and they would have seen their own unrighteousness. They would have then been prepared for Christ and the Gospel.

Jesus taught them the correct interpretation of the Law (Matthew 5:17-28). But even though Jesus taught them to understand what God's laws really meant, the Jewish leaders would not allow the Law to judge and condemn them. If they had, they would have been broken in heart and truly repentant.

John the Baptist also gave the right interpretation of the Law as preparation for the Gospel. But the religious leaders rejected both the ministry of John the Baptist and of Jesus. Why? Because their correct interpretation of the Law exposed the true condition of the scribes' and Pharisees' hearts. They rejected this preparatory ministry of the Law, and therefore they rejected Christ and the Gospel of God's grace (Matthew 5:17-28).

Jesus' conversation with the woman of Samaria is yet another example of the necessity of preparing a person for the Gospel by the correct use of the Law. After Jesus had gained her attention by speaking about her felt need for water, He brought her face to face with her real need. Jesus said to her, *"Go, call your husband"* (John 4:16). Jesus knew this woman would never be prepared to trust only in the grace of God until she faced the truth that she had transgressed the Law which forbids adultery.

Jesus' method of dealing with the rich young ruler provides another lesson for us. Unless a person faces the truth about his sin and condemnation before a holy God, he will not recognize his need for the Gospel.

The rich young ruler, secure in his own apparent goodness and ability to keep the Law, came to Jesus and asked Him what he had to do to inherit eternal life (Mark 10:17-22). Through this young man's greeting, Jesus recognized immediately that he was a soul unprepared for the Gospel. This young ruler greeted Jesus as a fellow human being by saying, "Good Teacher." He had never been enlightened by the Law to realize that *"No one is good but One, that is, God."* He was unaware that all the goodness and righteousness of man, when judged in the light of the perfect goodness and righteousness of God, is nothing more than a bundle of filthy rags (Isaiah 64:6).

Because Jesus recognized this young man's lost condition and his lack of preparation for the Gospel, He did not offer him the grace and forgiveness of the Gospel. Jesus had not come to call a self-righteous, rich young ruler to repentance; He came to call sinners to repentance. Before this young man could understand that the Gospel of God's grace was the only way by which he could enter eternal life, he first had to be taught his sinfulness and unrighteousness in God's sight.

What did Jesus use to reveal this man's true heart condition? Did Jesus use some cultural felt need to lead him into genuine repentance? Did Jesus tell the young man, "Smile, God loves you?" Did He ignore his lack of conviction and immediately introduce him to some easy steps to eternal life? No! Jesus used the Law to expose the covetousness which held him captive.

Because this man had asked what he must do to inherit eternal life, Jesus told him what God required him to do. Being self-righteous, this man believed he could be saved by doing and didn't need God's mercy as a sinner. Therefore, Jesus quoted some of the Law to him.

The rich young ruler's response evidenced his lack of understanding of the perfection of God. He immediately claimed that he had kept these laws perfectly from childhood. Knowing this young man's true spiritual condition and his secret love of money, Jesus said, *"Go your way, sell whatever you have and give to the poor."* Through this command, Jesus was confronting this young man with the practical realities of the second great commandment, *"You shall love your neighbor as yourself"* (Mark 12:31).

Then Jesus said to this ruler, *"Come, take up the cross, and follow Me."* This command was based on the first great commandment, *"You shall love the LORD your God with all your heart, with all your soul, with all your mind, and with all your strength"* (Mark 12:30).

What was the young man's response? Did he turn and repent? Did he, like the publican in the temple, acknowledge that he was a sinner and needed God's mercy? No. He rejected the revealing, condemning ministry of the Law. He turned away, clutching his riches as his greatest treasure. He went away grieved, but apparently unrepentant for his covetousness. Those who reject the message of the Law cannot receive the Gospel.

The majority of the Jews rejected the preparatory work of the Law given through Moses and also taught by John the Baptist, Jesus, and the apostles. Even though they had received the written Law of God, they were self-righteous and trusted in a mere outward conformity to the Law. Because they clung to their self-righteousness, refusing to accept God's verdict on them, they were not prepared to come by faith alone and trust in the grace of God. In contrast, many of the Gentiles, who had been without the direct written message from God, accepted the condemnation of the Law and saw the reality of their spiritual bankruptcy. Therefore, they were ready to turn in faith to Christ and the Gospel as their only hope (Romans 3:19).

The hymn entitled "Jehovah Tsidkenu" was written by R. Murray M'Cheyne and is his testimony to the way the Lord taught and prepared him through the Law to see his need of the Savior. ("Jehovah Tsidkenu" means "Jehovah our Righteousness.")

I once was a stranger to grace and to God;
I knew not my danger, I felt not my load;
Though friends spoke in rapture of Christ on the tree,
JEHOVAH TSIDKENU was nothing to me.

When free grace awoke me by light from on high,
Then legal fears shook me, I trembled to die;
No refuge, no safety in self could I see,
JEHOVAH TSIDKENU my Saviour must be.

My terrors all vanished before the sweet Name;
My guilty fears banished, with boldness I came
To drink at the fountain, life-giving and free;
JEHOVAH TSIDKENU is all things to me.

The professing believers to whom I first ministered in the Philippines had never judged themselves according to the perfection and holiness of God as revealed in the Law. Because they had not been exposed to the correct ministry of the Law, they were trusting in a mixture of works and grace. They were offering God their own sacrifices of good works instead of accepting God's mercy in the Gospel of Christ.

Referring to the time in his life when he was one of the leading Pharisees, Paul said, *"I was alive once without the law, but when the commandment came, sin revived and I died"* (Romans 7:9). Paul was a self-righteous, self-dependent man. He did not see himself as being spiritually sick or needing a Savior. However, when God the Holy Spirit faced Paul with the holy and righteous claims of the Law, he realized he was unspiritual and a slave to sin (Philippians 3:4-9; Romans 7:14). Paul wrote, *"Has then what is good become death to me? Certainly not! But sin, that it might appear sin, was producing death in me through what is good, so that sin through the commandment might become exceedingly*

sinful" (Romans 7:13). Because Paul had been prepared by the Law, he was ready to trust only in Christ.

As long as people are ignorant of the perfect righteousness of God, they will endeavor to save themselves through their own imperfect righteousness. Paul said of his own countrymen, *"For they being ignorant of God's righteousness, and seeking to establish their own righteousness, have not submitted to the righteousness of God"* (Romans 10:3).

If a person is ignorant of the righteousness of God, then he will go about trying to establish his own righteousness. Once he sees the holiness and righteousness of God as revealed by the Law, however, he will completely abandon any trust in his own goodness as a basis for acceptance by God. Once a person has been enlightened by the Holy Spirit through the Word of God, he will say, "If that is what God is like and if he demands perfection from me, then I give up. I will no longer try to merit His favor by what I do. I am unable to obey His holy commands and so please Him." Then, and only then, is a person's heart ready to receive the good news that *"when we were still **without strength**, in due time Christ died for the ungodly"* (Romans 5:6).

Our responsibility

Today, in most evangelical circles, the usual practice is to present some verses and evidences of man's need and then swiftly turn to the Gospel. Following this quick presentation of man's need, a great deal of time is spent endeavoring to persuade the hearers to turn to Christ. Our great mistake is turning quickly to the remedy without spending sufficient time preparing people for the Gospel.

Because Western society to a large degree has maintained a facade of Christianity, most Christian workers presume that people already have the foundations for the Gospel. We assume they already have a basic understanding of God and His nature and character. However, the vast majority of people in so-called Christian countries have little biblical knowledge of God. Of the relatively few in our countries who do attend church, most have a humanistic and unscriptural concept of God. Regardless of this tremendous lack, the average preacher spends little time on this all-important, basic subject.

It is small wonder that there is little respect for God and spiritual matters in our day. All true spiritual revivals and movements of the Spirit of God have been the result of the acknowledgment of who God really is. This alone brings true contrition of heart, genuine repentance, faith, worship and holy living. If evangelists and preachers spent more time teaching about the true nature and character of God, and less time trying to convince sinners of the advantages of coming to God, we would hear the question asked more often by repentant, anxious sinners, *"Sirs, what must I do to be saved?"* (Acts 16:30).

While we may agree that there must be a preparatory work done in the heart of a sinner before he will trust only in Christ, some may be of the opinion that this is God's sovereign work in which we have no part. It is clear from the Scriptures that God prepares man's heart through His Word. *"'Is not My word like a fire?' says the LORD, 'And like a hammer that breaks the rock in pieces?'"* (Jeremiah 23:29). The Holy Spirit uses the Word of God to convict the world of sin, of righteousness, and of judgment (John 16:8). God has entrusted us with the proclamation of His message (2 Corinthians 5:18-20).

We are responsible to prepare our hearers through the Scriptures by correctly applying the Law before we offer the Gospel to them. I remember beginning to teach a new weekly home Bible study with a couple in Australia. Before I started teaching that first night, the husband interrupted me and said, "Now, just a moment. Before you say anything, I have something to say."

"OK, go ahead," I replied.

He said, "I reckon that if a person keeps the Law and does exactly what it says, he will be all right and will be accepted by God."

When I agreed with him, his head almost swelled visibly. Turning to his wife, he bragged, "There you are. I told you so. That woman at the City Mission didn't know what she was talking about. She told me I couldn't be saved by what I did."

I told him, "I agree with what you said so I want to write it down." So I wrote down, "Wim said that if we obey the Law and do exactly what it says, God will accept us and we will be OK." Of course, at that point, Wim didn't realize that he did not have the ability to obey the Law, because he had been born a sinner. After I had written these words, I put the piece of paper in the front of my Bible. My plan was to produce it at an appropriate future date.

After a few months of weekly chronological Bible studies, beginning in the book of Genesis, we finally reached the story of the giving of the Law. It was obvious from Wim's questions and answers that the Lord was working in his life. As we continued studying the Law, giving the spiritual meaning and application of each of the commandments, Wim was listening carefully. Finally, one night, he interrupted my teaching and said, "I haven't got a hope. I break all of God's laws every day."

Praise God! Wim's spiritual eyes had been opened to see his own sinfulness and inability to please God by personal obedience to the Law. This knowledge had come to him through the study of the Old Testament stories and the Law, which revealed the holy and righteous character of God. Later, during our Bible studies, Wim saw that Christ alone had kept the Law and, through His death, had provided a way of salvation for sinful, helpless sinners.

What would have been the result if I had given the Gospel at the beginning of our Bible study, without first exposing Wim to the demands of God's holy Law? Wim would not have clearly understood the absolute necessity of the Gospel. He was not prepared for the Gospel. He felt no need for the grace and mercy of God. He was self-righteous and therefore self-dependent. Possibly, he would have professed faith in Christ, but in his heart, he would have still been dependent on his own efforts and self-righteousness.

Not only has the Gospel been committed to us, but the preparation of souls for the Gospel has also been committed to us. We need to take this seriously. Paul wrote to Timothy, *"We know that the law is good if one uses it lawfully, knowing this: that the law is not made for a righteous person, but for the lawless and insubordinate ... according to the glorious gospel of the blessed God which was committed to my trust"* (1 Timothy 1:8-9, 11). Paul knew that the Gospel would not be meaningful without the right application of the Law. The right use of the Law is the means to prepare sinners for the Gospel. The Law is God's appointed schoolmaster to lead the self-righteous to Christ.

We should, through the correct use of the Law, bring people to see that they need a righteousness equal to the righteousness of God, for only that will satisfy a holy God. The question then arises, "Where can I find this righteousness which will satisfy God? How can God be satisfied with me? I have broken His Law. I am condemned to everlasting punishment. How can my debt of sin be paid? How can I be justified and declared righteous before my perfect Judge?"

While some are of the opinion that this preparatory work is the sovereign responsibility of God, others believe that the Gospel should be immediately preached to all, regardless of their lack of preparation, because the Gospel is the power of God unto salvation. They believe the Gospel will prepare the sinner's heart and also save his soul. The Gospel is indeed the power of God unto salvation, but to whom? Romans 1:16 says it is the power of God unto salvation *"for everyone who believes."* Who will trust only in the Gospel and be saved? Only those whose hearts have been prepared like the good soil – those who have been convicted and prepared by God and have been taught by the Holy Spirit to agree with God about their sin, Christ's righteousness, and God's coming judgment (John 16:8-11).

One Sunday morning, a Palawano woman came to our house for the first time. Many years earlier, she had heard some of the Word of God, but for a long time, there hadn't been any missionaries in her area. We had just built a house and had started teaching God's Word in a location about a two or three hours' walk from her home. She came to see us and said excitedly, "I have been out of God for 10 years, but now I want to come back into God." By this term "out of God," she meant that she hadn't been attending Christian meetings and doing all the things she associated with being a Christian. By the term "come back into God," she indicated that she was going to attend the meetings once again, sing, pray, and listen to the teaching of God's Word.

I talked with this woman on several occasions about Christ and His death for sinners, and I asked her about her own personal faith in Christ and His death. She said, "Yes, I am trusting in Christ." Nevertheless, her emphasis was on the fact that she had at one time been in God, had been baptized, and that she knew many hymns and prayed. She no longer had a New Testament, but she wanted another one because she was coming back into God. Unless specifically asked, however, she never spoke about the death of Christ for sinners.

I said to her, "All of the things you speak of are good in their place, but they will not save you. Only Christ can save you." Again and again when speaking to her, I emphasized Christ's death for sinners.

She answered, "Oh, yes, the previous missionary told me He died. Yes, I believe that."

I thought, "Maybe she is truly saved."

When she returned a week or two later, she said, "I am so happy to be able to sing the hymns, pray, and attend meetings. I am so glad to be back in God."

Once again, I reminded her of Christ's death as the only way back to God.

She answered, "Yes, I remember that." But then she asked the new believers in the area if they had been baptized. When they said that they had not been baptized, she told them that they hadn't even started on the way.

Each time she visited and boasted of her good works, I reminded her about Christ's death as the only way to God. From her attitude, it was clear that Christ's death was not meaningful to her. It seemed as if she thought, "I will be all right if I can only remember that part about Christ dying for sins and rising again."

On several occasions, my wife heard me reminding this woman of Christ's death for sinners. Finally, Fran said to me, "I can't understand you. You are doing the very thing you would tell other people not to do."

I questioned, "What's that?"

She replied, "You keep telling that woman the Gospel, but she is not prepared for the Gospel. She doesn't understand her need of the Gospel. She is not thirsty. She is not hungry. Her heart is not prepared for the Gospel."

My wife was right. I determined that when this Palawano woman returned, I would not remind her again of the Gospel. She needed to be taught the Law in order for her to comprehend her great need of Christ, and Christ alone, as her righteousness.

Shortly after this, she returned. I sat down to talk with her at about one o'clock in the afternoon. I began in Genesis and reminded her of the main stories in the Old Testament which provide the foundations for the doctrine of God, man and sin. Because she had been attending the meetings, she needed only to be reminded of most of these stories.

As we went through the stories, I emphasized the holiness of God, His hatred of sin, man's sinfulness, and especially the fact that God's Law requires death as the payment for sin. I wanted to make it clear to her that God would accept no compromise. I applied these truths to her personally by telling her that baptism, hymn singing, church attendance, reading the Scriptures, or any other thing that she could do would not pay for her sin.

About five o'clock that afternoon, she was frustrated and desperate and began to cry. Although Palawanos do not like to be seen crying publicly, she cried because she was so overcome by the hopelessness of her position before God.

While she was crying, I was silently praying, "Lord, give me wisdom. What should I say to her? I don't want her to mentally agree with what I have shared from your Word but not trust only in Your Son and the Gospel. Lord, save this woman! Bring her to that place where she sees her salvation is only in Christ, so she will put her faith in Him and never again in herself or anything that she can do."

Finally, I said to her, "God requires death, but isn't there somewhere you can find the payment instead of you dying? Isn't there someone who could pay it? I can't pay it for you because I, too, deserve to be separated from God because of my sins."

For a time, we sat there in silence. Finally, she looked up at me through her tears and answered, "Jesus."

Joyfully, I replied, "Yes, Jesus. He's the only One."

That woman's whole attitude was changed from that time. Gone was her boasting and trust in anything else except the Lord Jesus Christ. How sweet the name of Jesus sounds to a believer's ear! He is the answer.

Christian, it will thrill your soul, if, through the correct teaching of the nature and character of God and the Law of God, you give the Holy Spirit the opportunity to prepare people for the Gospel, for then they will trust only in the Lord Jesus as the One who died for them and fully satisfied God on their behalf.

5

Divine Building Principles

During our early years with the Palawanos many came to understand justification by faith through God's grace. Many who had previously been mere professors of salvation were saved, and others received assurance and clarity regarding their personal salvation. Not only was I teaching justification by faith, but other missionaries among the Palawanos had also realized the true condition of the Palawan churches and were endeavoring to strengthen the basic foundations of the people's faith. What a thrill to see the people trusting in Christ alone!

How could these babes in Christ best be nurtured and fed? With so many people to teach, I felt like a doctor dispensing vitamins to an undernourished and starving people. Our itinerant teaching program was totally inadequate to meet the needs of these young believers and build them up in the faith. Therefore, I decided to switch from a predominantly topical teaching approach to verse-by-verse exposition. I relocated my family to the middle of an area with six small churches and began to give these Palawano churches concentrated expositional teaching.

Because the congregations of these six churches were a mixture of saved, mere professors, and a few who didn't even claim to be children of God, I started teaching expositionally through the Gospel according to John. Starting with great enthusiasm, it soon became apparent that my hearers were not ready for an expositional study of John. They could not understand any of the verses containing direct references or allusions to people or stories from the Old Testament, because they had never been taught the basic Old Testament historical sequence of events as one complete story.

The following examples show a few of the problems I encountered:

- John 1:1, *"In the beginning was the Word."* Even though the people may have heard about the beginning from previous missionaries, it was vague and uncertain in their minds. So I had to go back to Genesis 1 and teach about the beginning of time.

- John 1:1, *"And the Word was with God."* After explaining that the Word is yet another title for the Lord Jesus, it was obvious that the Palawano people did not understand that Jesus was with the Father before the beginning.

- John 1:3, *"All things were made through Him."* The people did not understand that God in Genesis 1 was three Persons – God the Father, God the Son, and God the Spirit.

- John 1:11, *"He came to His own."* This meant little to the Palawanos without the background of the call of Abraham, the Messianic promises, and the history of Israel.

- John 1:14, *"And the Word became flesh and dwelt among us, and we beheld His glory."* This alludes to the Old Testament tabernacle and the Shekinah glory wherein God lived in the midst of Israel. The Palawanos didn't know these stories.

- John 1:17, *"The law was given through Moses."* The people had insufficient knowledge of the chronology of the Bible story, and they didn't know where the Old Testament and New Testament characters fit in the sequence of events. They questioned if Moses and John the Baptist were contemporaries, and wondered if Jesus was on the earth at the same time as the people mentioned from the Old Testament.

As these few examples show, the Gospel according to John is full of references to the Old Testament. Due to the Palawanos' sketchy understanding of the Old Testament, I had to intermittently break off the exposition of the book of John in order to teach the Old Testament story or truth to which John referred or alluded. This piecemeal form of teaching was frustrating for me as the teacher and confusing for my hearers.

I was forced to conclude that a clearer and less complicated way to teach the Scriptures must exist. A major forward step had been made when I turned from predominantly teaching topically to direct verse-by-verse exposition of the New Testament books. Nevertheless, it was now apparent that choosing any book and teaching it expositionally was not the complete answer to teaching the Scriptures clearly. What was the answer?

One book

The Scriptures were written with a definite beginning and a definite ending. Between the beginning and ending are incidents which, when taught and understood in their historical sequence,

form one complete, cohesive, intelligible story. If one were to teach the contents of any other book, he would naturally start at the beginning and follow the forward movement of the subject as the author develops and brings it to its logical conclusion. Little wonder we had difficulties when teaching the New Testament to the Palawanos!

Previously, I had approached the Bible as a book which contained the message of the Gospel. I now began to consider the Bible holistically – as God's complete, unified message to all mankind. I realized the Old Testament is not a compilation of interesting stories to be used only as types which pointed forward to Christ or illustrations of New Testament truth. The Old Testament is the logical introduction, foundation and authority for the story of Christ recorded in the New Testament. The Old Testament is by far the most important source of interpretive background material for the historical accounts of the New Testament. Just as God has given us two lips, and both are necessary for clear verbal communication, even so both Old and New Testaments are indispensable for the communication of God's complete message to the world.

One story

The whole Bible is God's message about His Son, the Savior. God's chief purpose in writing His Book was to reveal Christ. The Old Testament is the preparation for Christ. The New Testament is the manifestation of Christ. The Scriptures reveal Christ from Genesis to Revelation. Jesus said to the Jews of His day, *"You search the Scriptures, for in them you think you have eternal life; and these are they which testify of Me"* (John 5:39). The entire Scriptures find their meaning in the Lord Jesus Christ. Jesus Christ is the origin, the substance, and the object of all divine revelation.

His-story, that is, the story of Christ, begins in the first verse of Genesis, for He was there in the beginning. At the fall of man, the Son of the virgin is promised – One who will overcome

Satan and deliver his captives. The story of Christ then continues through the entire Old Testament in numerous types and prophecies. The New Testament records the fulfillment of these prophecies through His birth, life, death, ascension and present glory. The story of Christ, as told in the Gospels, is the sequel to the Old Testament.

The book of Matthew opens with the story of the birth of Christ, not as the beginning of the story but as the fulfillment and consummation of all that was written previously. Matthew connects the story of Christ with Abraham, to whom God had given the promise, *"In you all the families of the earth shall be blessed"* (Genesis 12:3). This, and all the other promises given to Abraham, were to be fulfilled through Abraham's Seed, *"who is Christ"* (Galatians 3:16).

The book of Mark launches almost directly into the life of Christ, but Mark is nonetheless careful to remind his readers that this story is not the beginning but the fulfillment of that which was *"written in the Prophets"* (Mark 1:2).

Luke traces the genealogy of Christ to Adam (Luke 3:23-38). By doing this, Luke shows us that the story which he wrote cannot be understood by reading only of Mary and Joseph or of Jesus born as a babe in Bethlehem. To clearly understand Luke's account, we must also be aware of Adam's part as the first man in the historical drama of the Bible.

John tells the ongoing story of the Word. The story of the Word begins in eternity. It continues in the Word's creation of all things and then in His incarnation (John 1:1-3). The future story of the Word is told in the Revelation, where He is described as being *"clothed with a robe dipped in blood"* (Revelation 19:13).

When Jesus saw the need to explain the necessity of His death to two sadly disillusioned men on the road to Emmaus, He turned back to the Old Testament, *"And beginning at Moses [Genesis to Deuteronomy] and all the Prophets*

[the remainder of the Old Testament], *He expounded to them in all the Scriptures the things concerning Himself"* (Luke 24:27).

The Christ-story cannot be clearly taught or understood apart from its God-given beginnings found only in the Old Testament. Therefore, it is our responsibility to teach the beginnings in the Old Testament and then teach the fulfillment in the New Testament. In the Old Testament, God has given types which so clearly point forward to Christ, and redemptive analogies to prepare people to understand the New Testament story of Christ. These Old Testament types of Christ and redemptive analogies point to and interpret the birth, life, death, burial and resurrection of the Lord Jesus Christ.

Biblical redemptive analogies

Instead of emphasizing the Old Testament redemptive analogies as the basis for the understanding of the Christ-story, some missionaries seem to depend more on redemptive analogies found in the cultures of various ethnic groups.

A young missionary en route to his homeland for furlough passed through Australia. As I talked to him, it became obvious that he was discouraged with the lack of progress in his missionary work. When I asked if he had presented the Gospel to the people, he told me that he hadn't. My next inquiry was why he had been such a long time in the tribe but had not yet begun to evangelize. The reason he gave was that, in spite of all his searching, he had failed to find the cultural redemptive analogy or what he thought was the God-given key for their clear understanding and acceptance of the Gospel. Because he failed to find the key or redemptive analogy, he didn't have confidence to preach the Gospel to those lost tribal people. Since he was returning to the USA, I asked him what the redemptive analogy or God-given key to open the door to understand salvation is in the American culture. Because he didn't know, I replied, "According to what you believe, it won't be of any use for you to tell your fellow Americans the Gospel until you find the key."

If God has placed such an effective medium of blessing within some cultures, then surely we can expect that the Lord has placed them in all. If God has indeed given redemptive analogies which are hidden within the cultures of primitive peoples to serve as the keys to open their understanding to accept the Bible, God, Christ and salvation, then we must never cease in our search. But how will we know when we have found the right key? Who will be the judge? What will be our criterion or standard of judgment? If we come to the conclusion that we have found the key because we see tribal people understanding and accepting the Gospel, how do we know there is not yet another even more suitable key prepared by God and waiting to be used to unlock the cultural door for an even greater movement to God and the Gospel?

Cultural stories and rituals, which resemble or illustrate Bible stories and Old Testament rituals and ceremonies, can be useful in explaining the Gospel but they are not the God-given keys to open the people's understanding of the Gospel. These stories and rituals are most likely remnants of the truth which the whole human race knew before the dispersion at the tower of Babel. They have been passed down orally in many primitive societies and have been greatly changed and grossly distorted. The truth of God once known has been deliberately set aside for the lies of Satan (Romans 1:18-32). One of the clearest illustrations of this would be the widespread use of blood as a way of appeasement and sacrifice. This knowledge originated with the blood sacrifices which God ordained after the fall of man. Blood sacrifices, once commanded by God as the only way of approach to Him, are now used in many tribal cultures as sacrifices to Satan and evil spirits.

Missionaries should know all they can about the culture, folklore and beliefs of the people they are reaching for Christ, and they should use carefully selected illustrations and analogies when teaching God's Word. These, however, are not substitutes for the preparation of the hearts of sinners through the proclamation of the Scriptures. Cultural analogies and illustrations, regardless of their clarity, cogency, or incredible biblical parallelism, should never take precedence over the scriptural redemptive types and analogies. Cultural redemptive analogies are no substitute for the God-given redemptive analogies of the Old Testament, which so graphically typify Christ and His work of redemption. Some secret significance or evil connotation, of which the missionary may be totally unaware, may be hidden in cultural analogies. If the missionary depends too much on cultural analogies, rather than biblical analogies, he may unwittingly guide the people into grievous misunderstanding, error and syncretism. In addition, overemphasis on cultural redemptive analogies may cause the people to believe that the missionary is confirming and giving credence to their beliefs.

Jesus told the Pharisees that the truth of God's Word sets Satan's captives free from sin's bondage (John 8:32), and He declared in His prayer to His Father, *"Your word is truth"* (John 17:17). Paul charged Timothy to *"preach the word"* (2 Timothy 4:2). The living and enduring Word of God, the imperishable seed, when believed, results in souls being born again (1 Peter 1:23).

No evidence exists in the Scriptures to prove that God's Word is effectual for the release of tribal people from Satan's dominion only when interpreted by cultural redemptive analogies. God has provided us with spiritual weapons with which we are to fight Satan, demolish his strongholds, arguments and pretensions, which set themselves against the knowledge of God (2 Corinthians 10:3-5).

God's revelation for the world

The biblical redemptive analogies given by God to Israel were also for the whole world. *"For whatever things were written before were written for our learning, that we through the patience and comfort of the Scriptures might have hope"* (Romans 15:4). God has not spoken directly to the Gentiles, but He has chosen to speak to the Gentiles through His Word given to Israel and the Church. All people must come to God's light shining from the Scriptures. By the infinitely wise and sovereign appointment of God, all of the redemptive story and the beginning of the Church of Jesus Christ are set within the cultural, geographical and historical framework of the nation of Israel. Therefore, no one can clearly understand the story of the New Testament without a basic knowledge of Israel's origin, development and history from the Old Testament.

The Lord created the nation of Israel for Himself, so that He could use it as His witness and channel of blessing to all of mankind (Isaiah 43:1, 10-12, 21). The Lord's promises to Abraham, the father of the nation of Israel, indicated that God's blessings through him and his seed would extend to *"all the families of the earth"* (Genesis 12:1-3). This promise was fulfilled through Christ, the promised Seed, but also through the Scriptures, entrusted to Israel as the only revelation of God to the world. All other nations were left in ignorance, without God and without hope, unless they were willing to accept the truth and wisdom given through God's chosen channel, Israel. The Lord said to Israel, *"You only have I known of all the families of the earth"* (Amos 3:2). In contrast, the Gentile nations, prior to Pentecost, are spoken of as *"a people I have not known"* (Psalm 18:43).

The Bible alone is God's revelation to the world. This is the foundational truth of Christianity. A major cause for the growth of Buddhism, Hinduism, Islam, and many other false religions in societies once strongly influenced by the Judeo-Christian faith can be attributed to the writings of liberal and modern writers. Although some of these writers claim to be Christians, they teach that truth is not limited to the Hebrew-Christian Scriptures but is also found in the writings of other world religions. Animistic people believe that truth is based on folklore and revelations from the spirits.

The Christian missionary's responsibility is to clearly establish, through teaching the Scriptures, that God's revelation of truth for all people was given through no other nation except Israel and those men appointed by God to write the New Testament. Therefore, if the nations and peoples of the world are to know the truth and the blessings of God, they, too, must turn to the Bible as the only genuine and complete divine revelation. This revelation of God began with the Old Testament and was completed with the New Testament revelation in and through Israel's Messiah, Jesus of Nazareth. *"God, who at various times and in various ways spoke in time past to the fathers by the prophets, has in these last days spoken to us by His Son, whom He has appointed heir of all things, through whom also He made the worlds"* (Hebrews 1:1-2).

The Bible then is one book. The Old Testament is the introduction and only sound basis for the understanding and interpretation of the New Testament story concerning Christ and His redemptive work.

But has God only told us what to teach and left how we teach up to us? As my search continued, it became clear that the Lord wrote the Scriptures not only to tell us what to teach, but also to demonstrate principles and guidelines as to how we should teach His message to the world. His methods of teaching are the best; and He means for us to study and be guided by them when we teach His Word to others.

The literary form of the Bible

God is the greatest teacher, and all intelligent beings are His pupils. No one can escape from His classroom, the universe. The angels, and even Satan and his demons, are subject to God's divine teaching process (Ephesians 3:10). The voice of

God is heard in innumerable ways throughout all creation.

Man, created on earth by God and for God, was intended to be the willing pupil of God. God's voice of wisdom says, *"To you, O men, I call, and my voice is to the sons of men. O you simple ones, understand prudence, and you fools, be of an understanding heart"* (Proverbs 8:4-5).

The omniscient Teacher wrote a Book to teach and lead mankind into the full understanding of truth about Himself and His perfect will for all created beings. Because He created man, He understands perfectly the functions of man's mind. God knows how best to captivate the human imagination and lead people to a clear comprehension of truth.

The author of a book must decide what literary style he considers most suitable for his subject and his readers. The author of children's books must approach his subject in a form suitable for his topic, considering the limitations of a child's mind; whereas a person writing for adults must choose a method of presentation suitable for the topic of his book and the intelligence of its prospective adult readers.

The divine Teacher, perfectly knowing His subject matter and human pupils, chose the most suitable literary style for His Book. This Book has been entrusted to the Church, the Body of Christ. The Church, God's representative on earth, was given the Bible to take God's message of reconciliation to the world (2 Corinthians 5:18-20). Nevertheless, the Church has generally acted like a teacher who, having been given a well-prepared teaching manual, ignores the method and style of presentation chosen by the author and completely revamps and reorganizes the subject matter in his own teaching format. In most cases, teachers of the Scripture in every department of the Church, from the Sunday School to the mission field, have failed to consider and follow God's form of teaching so clearly demonstrated in His teaching manual, the Bible.

History

That which God recorded in the Scriptures actually happened in time and space. God spoke. God acted. God interacted with real, historical human beings. The contents of the Bible are relevant to all people in every age, regardless of their culture, because the Bible is a book of case histories. We are able to identify with those people whose lives are recorded in the Bible. God interacted and spoke to real people – people like us.

God has revealed Himself through His acts in history. When God needed to remind Israel of His true identity, He pointed them back to His historical relationship with their forefathers. The Lord said to Moses, *"Thus you shall say to the children of Israel: 'The LORD God of your fathers, the God of Abraham, the God of Isaac, and the God of Jacob, has sent me to you. This is My name forever"* (Exodus 3:15).

The Lord constantly reminded His chosen people, "If you wish to know who I am and what I am, then remember how I acted in relationship with your fathers Abraham, Isaac and Jacob. Remember how I acted in my relationship with you as a nation. Recollect how I delivered you out of Egypt. Look what I did to the Egyptians through the plagues which I brought on that sinful nation. Remember how I delivered you at the Passover and at the Red Sea. Don't forget how I treated you in the wilderness. Did any of My promises fail? Call to mind how I brought you into this land which I promised you. Remember that I brought judgment upon you because of your idolatry, and took you away into Assyria and Babylon, but restored you to your own land in fulfillment of My promises."

God revealed Himself as He walked through history with man. Cited in the Scriptures are numerous incidents relating to events in Israel's history through which God revealed His nature and character (Exodus 3:13-15; Deuteronomy 7:18-19; 8; 11:1-7; Psalms 105; 106; 111).

Because God actively revealed Himself within the context of the historical events recorded in the Scriptures, Israel's leaders and prophets constantly rehearsed and reminded the people of Israel of their history.

Israel's faith rested on God as revealed through His historical acts. This is seen in their continual remembrance of their deliverance by God out of Egypt at the time of the Passover. The faith of every generation was to be built on the firm foundation of the God of history who had revealed Himself as Israel's Redeemer on that memorable night in Egypt (Exodus 12:24-27). Each successive generation of Israelites was taught the historical facts regarding God's redemption of them as a people. Each individual Israelite had to exercise faith if he was to enter into the salvation of the Lord, but this faith was not in some personal, subjective experience. It was faith in the Lord of history, the Redeemer of their nation. As the Israelites participated by faith in the Passover celebrations, they were signifying their faith in the God of Israel, the God of redemption, the God of history, the God of Abraham, Isaac and Jacob. They looked to an historical event which had brought salvation to them as a nation. They knew and trusted in God as He had revealed Himself in history.

God has not only shown what He is like in action in the Old Testament, but also in the New Testament. When God planned to show mankind finally and completely what He is like, He stepped into history in the person of Jesus Christ, His Son. What did Jesus answer when Philip said, *"Lord, show us the Father, and it is sufficient for us"?* Jesus said, *"Have I been with you so long, and yet you have not known Me, Philip? He who has seen Me has seen the Father"* (John 14:8-9). The disciples needed to understand that Jesus was God in action. He was God – living, talking, walking, and speaking before them. If they wanted to see what God was like, they must look to, listen to, and believe on the Lord Jesus. *"No one has seen God at any time. The only begotten Son, who is in the bosom of the Father, He has declared Him"* (John 1:18).

God was in action in the Old Testament as Jehovah. God was in action in the New Testament as Jesus Christ. God was also in action in the Acts of the Apostles in the person of the Holy Spirit.

The apostles' emphasis

The apostles recognized the Old Testament as God's record of His involvement in the world, and especially with His chosen people, Israel, in preparation for the coming of the Savior. The Old Testament was the Bible of the early Church. The apostolic preaching recorded in Acts first emphasized God's historical acts in relationship to Abraham, Isaac, Jacob, Joseph, Moses, David, and the nation of Israel. The apostles then linked these acts of God in the Old Testament to the revelation of Himself in the history of His Son, Jesus of Nazareth. The apostles interpreted the whole of Christ's advent, life, death, resurrection, present glory, and all future revelations of His majesty on the basis of the historical accounts and prophecies of the Old Testament. They used the Old Testament to authenticate the claim of Jesus of Nazareth to be the Christ. For them, the story of Christ began long before they met Him beside the Sea of Galilee, or at the River Jordan where John was baptizing. The faith of the apostles, and those who believed the apostles' message, rested on the basis of the testimony given concerning the Christ from the Old Testament. They taught as one story the Old Testament and its history and the events which they had so recently experienced in the company of Jesus of Nazareth.

This method of teaching is clearly evident, beginning with Peter's sermon on the day of Pentecost. Another classic example is the sermon of Stephen, in which he gives an account of Old Testament history beginning with Abraham. Stephen climaxes his sermon with a brief account of the nation of Israel's attitude toward

God's final messenger, the Lord Jesus. Acts 8 records the story of Philip who met the Ethiopian eunuch when the latter was reading Isaiah 53. Philip linked this Old Testament portion of Scripture to the events which had so recently taken place at Golgotha, and brought this man to an understanding of the Gospel. (Note also Acts 2:22-36; 3:13-26; 7; 10:34-43; 13:16-41; 17:2-3.)

The Church's responsibility

The Old Testament Scriptures, which prepare the mind to see the need and purpose for the incarnation, have been badly neglected by the Church. Multitudes misinterpret the whole purpose of Christ's ministry and death because they have little, if any, understanding of the biblical reasons for His coming. If those who declare the Gospel in homes, churches, Bible studies, Sunday schools, and the greater world community were to teach the beginnings of the redemptive story from the Old Testament before they teach its fulfillment in the New Testament, many more would clearly understand the advent of Christ as God's plan for their salvation. But while Christians continue to ignore this divinely revealed order of teaching, the confusion in the minds of many concerning Christ and His mission will continue.

Of recent times, many missionaries, pastors, and other Christians have taken the time to teach people the Old Testament beginnings of the Christ-story and have carefully followed the unfolding historical drama to its consummation in the New Testament. Upon completion of this teaching program, these Bible teachers have testified to the great clarity in their hearers' understanding of their helpless and sinful condition and of Christ's full provision for their salvation through His death, burial and resurrection.

In contrast, many have launched almost immediately into the story of Christ with little preparation from the history of the Old Testament. Some, after many years, have found that their message was outwardly accepted but not truly understood.

Bob Goddard, Sr., wrote the following about the Paĩ Tavy Tera tribal people of Paraguay:

The Jesuit priests established colonies with many of these tribal people over 400 years ago. The Jesuits were banished by the political leaders, and the tribal colonies were abandoned. In those days, the Mamelucos of Brazil made raids into Paraguay and carried off many Indians as slaves.

The results of all this are reflected in the culture and religious beliefs of these Paĩ Tavy Tera people. Religiously, they are willing to accept God and Jesus Christ, as they did from the Catholics years ago. They simply add them to their innumerable list of gods which is continually increasing.

This was unknown to our missionaries when they first presented the Gospel to the Paĩ Tavy Teras. Since there were those who were willing to accept their teaching and professed to be Christians, it seemed there was progress. However, as the years passed and very little sign of the reality of changed lives was observed, it was found that they did not understand the Gospel.

A study of their culture and religion has brought us to the conclusion that we must begin with Genesis and lay a foundation upon which to build so that they can understand who God is, what sin is, how man fell through sin and can be saved only through faith in God's Son, Jesus Christ.

The God of Christianity is the God of history. The faith of Christians is based on God's great revelatory acts, beginning with God's acts of creation and culminating in the historic, redemptive acts of the Lord Jesus Christ in His birth, life, death, resurrection and ascension to glory. Therefore, it is our responsibility to teach His-story. Just as Israel's teachers kept the history of Israel, wherein God acted, alive in a real and meaningful way as the basis of the faith of all succeeding generations of Israelites, so we are to teach. Not only should we teach the New Testament history of God's redemptive acts in and through our Lord Jesus Christ, but also the Old Testament history wherein God revealed Himself as the God of creation, judgment and salvation. Just as each individual Israelite was to look back to God's actions in history as the basis of his faith, so must we. For example, to remind us of God's central act of history on which we rest our faith, we have been given the Lord's Supper. *"Christ, our Passover, was sacrificed for us"* (1 Corinthians 5:7).

The Church must teach the historical content of the Scriptures so that people will not look to some subjective, personal experience as their hope of salvation. They should look instead to the objective reality of the living God as He has revealed Himself in and through biblical history, and to Christ's historical redemptive experiences on their behalf (2 Corinthians 5:18-20). When the historical content of the Scriptures is ignored, people become absorbed with their own subjective experiences rather than with the objective historical saving experiences of Jesus Christ as their representative. What we teach and emphasize to our hearers will become the foundation and basis of their faith. If our emphasis is on personal experiences, the people will be looking to inner experience as the basis for their acceptance before God. But if our message is biblical history, culminating with God's historical saving work in Christ, their faith will depend on the reality of Christ's accomplishments for them, completely apart from themselves and their own experience. They will look to God's finished work in Christ on their behalf.

The message we are given in the Bible to take to the world is not a list of doctrines or topical points about God. What we declare is that which actually happened in time and space. It is real. It is factual. It is history. When we bypass or ignore the historical content of the Scriptures in which God has revealed Himself, and divorce the words of God from their historical context, we are overlooking God's basic form of revelation. Furthermore, we are robbing the Bible of its strongest argument and reason to be recognized and accepted by the world as the only authentic revelation of God. God has stepped into the world's history, not once, not twice, but repeatedly. God has acted. God has spoken. God has not left man without a witness. He has revealed Himself to man as He has walked through history, not only as the Jehovah of the Old Testament but also as Jesus Christ of the New Testament. This marks the basic difference between the Hebrew-Christian faith and all other world religions, both past and present.

When Christian theology is stripped of the historical acts of God and presented to the Muslim, the Buddhist, the animist, or adherents to other world religions as a list of doctrines, Christianity then appears to be a mere alternative – the Western man's philosophy of God. Furthermore, Christian doctrines, taken apart from their historical revelatory content, can be easily adopted and added to the existing, established concept of God and religion. The result is syncretism, a wedding of pagan and Christian doctrines.

The Bible proclaims that the God of history is the one and only Creator, almighty Judge, and Savior of the world (Isaiah 43:9-17). There is only one true historical religion, that is, the religion of the Bible which was revealed and guided through history by God Himself. All other religions are false and are the deceiving work of Satan. The greatest safeguard against syncretism, misunderstanding, spurious converts, and an experience-oriented religion is the teaching of the Word of God as God has given it with all of its historical content. Therefore, we must not teach a set of doctrines divorced from their God-given historical setting; but rather, we must teach the story of the acts of God as He has chosen to reveal Himself in history. People may ignore our set of doctrines as our Western philosophy of God, but the story of God's actions in history cannot be refuted.

God uses this biblical, historical presentation of Himself to convince people of the truth of the Scriptures. Through this, people understand and are convinced that the God of Christians was not created through the speculations and vivid imaginations of Hebrew or Christian philosophers. Instead they can understand and believe that He is indeed the living, personal God who was and is involved in the history of the whole world. He is the God who is here. He is the God who knows them personally and knew their ancestors, even though they had never heard about Him (Acts 17:24-29). It is particularly important for people of other cultures to understand that the Christian God did not originate in the mind of some Western religious leader and that He is not the invented product of the Christian religion.

This then should be the content of our message to the nations, for this has been entrusted to us by God. Through teaching, we are to make all men aware of God's acts in history wherein He has revealed Himself. These historical revelations are for all people and have been recorded and preserved by God as the basis for saving faith.

6

Building Blocks in Evangelism

In 1962, the Lord had used Paul's ambition *"And so I have made it my aim to preach the gospel, not where Christ was named, lest I should build on another man's foundation"* (Romans 15:20) to challenge me to leave full-time evangelism in Australia. As a result, God led us to the Palawano tribal people where He also began to show me that people's hearts needed to be adequately prepared to hear the Gospel. In 1973, while still ministering among the Palawano, God used this verse once again to challenge me to go to a new area in Palawan which was without a Gospel witness. There, I was eager to put into practice the biblical principles God had taught me.

As I prepared to begin this new work farther south, I had some trepidation. Would I find after a few years that my methods and teaching produced the same misunderstanding of the Gospel, syncretism, legalism, and inadequate Old Testament foundation for the understanding of the New Testament with which I had grappled for so many years among the Palawano churches? What needed to be included in my evangelistic teaching program to prevent such misunderstanding?

It had become clear to me that when evangelizing one should follow the teaching guidelines demonstrated in the Scriptures. These teaching principles have been discussed in the previous chapters. In order to consider the logical and biblical reason for the teaching program which I am about to introduce, a brief summary is in order.

1. The Scriptures taught in evangelism must expose our hearers to the revelation of God's nature and character in order to prepare them for the Gospel. When evangelizing, one should teach in such a way that the hearers will judge themselves in the light of the biblical concept of God.

2. Because God chose to reveal Himself through His acts in history rather than by mere declarations and propositions, our evangelistic teaching must include the historical sections of Scripture wherein God has shown His true nature and character.

3. The Law must be part of our teaching as we prepare hearts to trust only in Christ, for *"by the law is the knowledge of sin"* (Romans 3:20). If we want to avoid syncretism, legalism, and a mixture of works and grace, we must use the Law in the correct way so that the consciences of our hearers will be exposed to the Law's convicting and convincing power.

4. The goal of all true evangelism is to see people trusting only in the Lord Jesus Christ and His

saving work on their behalf. If our hearers are to understand and correctly interpret the story of the Gospels concerning Christ, we should provide adequate Old Testament Christological background information.

5. During evangelism, our hearers should be taught the basic history and culture of Israel, for only then will they be able to understand the story of the Jewish Messiah, the Old Testament redemptive types which Christ fulfilled, Christ's position as the Son of David, King, and righteous Judge of Israel, His specific ministry to the lost sheep of Israel, and His final rejection by His own people.

The Lord had taught me that these biblical teaching guidelines are essential when evangelizing. How then could I be sure that all of these necessary aspects would be included in my evangelistic teaching program? Where could I find a teaching format which included each biblical teaching principle?

Considering each principle brought me to the conclusion that the best way to evangelize is to begin in the beginning and teach chronologically through the Scriptures to ensure that people understand the story of Christ and are properly prepared for the Gospel.

This first section of the Chronological Teaching Outline, which is for evangelism

and emphasizes salvation, begins in Genesis and concludes with the ascension of Christ, as recorded in the book of Acts. (See Figure 6-1.)

Evangelism for unbelievers

The Old Testament Scriptures provide the foundational revelation of God. God is sovereign, omnipotent, omniscient, omnipresent, holy, loving, righteous, merciful and immutable. God is man's Creator, Lawgiver, Judge and Savior. This revelation of God begins in Genesis 1 and continues through the historical development of the human race and through the lives of the patriarchs, beginning with Abraham. God's nature and character are further revealed by His judgments on Pharaoh and Egypt, the deliverance of Israel from slavery, and God's care for the Israelites in their journey to Mount Sinai. The Lord's sovereign position as man's Creator, Lawgiver and Judge is solemnly reinforced by the giving of the written Law. The disclosure of God's nature and character continues through His judgments on rebellious Israel, tempered by His mercy and ever-watchful preserving care. Through the ministries of Moses, Joshua, the judges, the kings and the prophets, God fully manifested that it is His prerogative to condemn the guilty and forgive the repentant.

The Old Testament covers the dispensation of Law. This does not mean that the grace of God was

Old Testament	Gospels	Acts	Epistles
Evangelism: *Firm Foundations: Creation to Christ* Designed to teach: Unbelievers Mixed groups with both unbelievers and believers Believers who have not studied this section of the curriculum			

Figure 6-1

not exhibited during the Old Testament era. The salvation of sinners, beginning with Adam and Eve, has ever and only been through the infinite grace of God. But even though the grace of God is evident in the Old Testament, the sovereignty, righteousness, holiness and judgment of God are even more noticeable. Through the Law given to Israel, God revealed Himself as the Holy One who will not condone sin or allow it to go unpunished. God's Law was given during the Old Testament era to expose the innate depravity of the human heart and God's holy anger against all who break His commandments. Therefore, there is no better or more straightforward way to bring an unsaved person face to face with the demands of God's holy Law than to expose him to the Old Testament portions in which God used the Law to teach and prepare the Israelites to see their helplessness and need of a Savior (Romans 3:19-20).

Is it necessary to teach all of the Old Testament to unsaved people before teaching them the life and saving work of Christ? No! It is quite unnecessary, for the greater part of the Old and New Testaments is addressed to believers. The main purpose of the Gospels, on the other hand, was to lead unsaved people into the knowledge of Christ's life and work of redemption. John said in his account, *"these are written that you may believe that Jesus is the Christ, the Son of God, and that believing you may have life in His name"* (John 20:31). It logically follows that, when evangelizing, one need only teach those portions of the Old Testament which are the foundations for the story of Christ from His birth to His ascension. Sufficient of the Old Testament story should be taught so that when Old Testament historical and geographical data, prophecies, personalities and illustrations are referred to or are used as illustrations by the Gospel writers, the hearers will already know the stories and so be able to clearly understand the meaning of and reason for the reference.

Following the flow of biblical history

Because God has chosen to reveal Himself within the framework of history, the Scriptures will be most clearly taught if we follow the flow of history from Genesis to Revelation.

The Chronological Teaching Outline presented in this book is based on the historical sections of the books of the Bible which record this forward movement of history. (See Figure 6-2.)

It takes too long to teach

One of the most common complaints regarding the form of teaching suggested in this book is that it takes too long to teach.

This is the day of speed and easy ways to do everything. Precooked frozen meals, instant desserts, and microwave ovens help make sure everything is on the table in a matter of minutes. Every conceivable gadget to speed up the process of daily living is available.

The same type of thinking has made inroads into the Christian church and is often applied to evangelism, church growth, and every other area of church life. The easy, quick and popular way is preferred to the longer method of systematically teaching the Scriptures. The quick method may appear to bring rapid results, but like seed in the Parable of the Sower that fell on unprepared ground, the unprepared professors soon fall away (Proverbs 21:5).

While Christians should be open to learn more efficient and effective ways to do their work, they must never forget that God's power is manifested and His work accomplished by the declaration of God's truth in the power of the Holy Spirit. There is no other way. God does not change His methods to fit in with modern thought and so-called advancements. *"For I am the LORD, I do not change"* (Malachi 3:6). This is true of

The Flow of Biblical History	
The Books of Historical Movement	**Other Books Written During these Periods**
Genesis	Job, Psalms
Exodus	Leviticus, Psalms
Numbers	Deuteronomy, Psalms
Joshua	Psalms
Judges	Ruth, Psalms
1 and 2 Samuel	Psalms
1 and 2 Kings	Proverbs, Ecclesiastes, Song of Solomon, 1 and 2 Chronicles, Isaiah, Hosea, Joel, Amos, Obadiah, Jonah, Micah, Nahum, Habakkuk, Zephaniah, Psalms
Daniel	Jeremiah, Lamentations, Ezekiel
Ezra	Haggai, Zechariah
Nehemiah	Esther
Malachi	
Matthew, Mark, Luke, John	
Acts	James, 1 and 2 Thessalonians, Galatians, 1 and 2 Corinthians, Romans, Philemon, Ephesians, Colossians, Philippians, 1 and 2 Peter, 1 and 2 Timothy, Titus, Hebrews, Jude, 1, 2 and 3 John
Revelation	

Figure 6-2

God's nature, and it is also true of His ways of working.

Man's greatest need is to hear, understand, and respond to the pure Word of God. God's power is inherent in His Word. It was through His Word that Almighty God brought order out of chaos, light out of darkness, and life to a lifeless world. And it is by His Word that the Lord exposes the wickedness of the human heart, brings life to the dead spirit of man, delivers Satan's captives, and gives sight to the spiritually blind (Isaiah 55:10-11; Luke 4:18; John 8:32; 1 Peter 1:23-25).

The Christian's responsibility is to teach God's Word in total dependence upon the Holy Spirit. No amount of human wisdom, ingenuity, or high-pressure evangelistic methods can hasten the work of the Holy Spirit and the conversion of a soul. It is not our responsibility to determine or try to force the time of the new birth. We are to faithfully teach all that has been committed to us and leave the work of transformation to the Lord.

One of the greatest faults in the ministry of the Church worldwide is the unwillingness to take the time to teach unsaved people over a long period of time and allow God the Holy Spirit to do His work of enlightening, convicting, and leading people to the type of faith in the Lord Jesus Christ, which will give them the assurance to say with Paul, *"I know whom I have believed and am persuaded that He is able to keep what I have committed to Him until that Day"* (2 Timothy 1:12).

Jack Douglas, missionary to the Pawaia tribe in Papua New Guinea, commented, "To teach right through from Genesis took a long time and much effort, but it was well worth it. The Pawaians know what they believe and why."

Most witnessing programs lead Christians into brief, face-to-face encounters with the unsaved. Insufficient effort is put into preparing the non-Christian to either understand the real reasons for, or the meaning of, the Gospel. Usually, just a few verses, such as Romans 3:23, are quoted to the unsaved and the person is then urged to make his or her decision for Christ.

The Scriptures make it clear that one person may be given the responsibility by God to sow the seed, another to water it, and yet another may reap the harvest (John 4:36-38; 1 Corinthians 3:6-7). In most methods of evangelism today, the person who sows is also expected to reap immediately. Truly the Lord is not limited. His Word is mighty to save, and He often does use the same person to both sow and reap. But our responsibility is to be sure that we are faithfully preaching all He has told us from His Word so that people are scripturally prepared for the Gospel. Then we can trust Him to give the increase.

The most effective witnessing programs are those which allow Christians to teach God's Word systematically and to depend upon the Holy Spirit

to do the work in His time. God's children should get to know unsaved people, establish Bible studies in their homes and teach consistently, even over weeks or months, those things which God has recorded in His Word as the foundations for the Gospel.

Tell the Gospel to the prepared

I have already given the reasons why the basic structure of the Old Testament should be taught to unsaved people before they are taught the New Testament story of Christ and the Gospel. But it must not be inferred that I am suggesting that no person can be saved until he has heard and understood all of the Old Testament outline presented in this teaching program. Nor am I saying that the teacher must not give the Gospel to a person prepared for the Gospel until he has been taught the proposed outline. We must not be bound by an outline, but we should be guided by biblical principles which are clearly taught throughout the entire Word of God.

If, at any point during the teaching of the Old Testament outline, an individual in a group of people is spiritually enlightened to his lost condition before God, the teacher will need the spiritual discernment to know when he should give that awakened sinner further private teaching on the birth, life, death and resurrection of the Lord Jesus Christ. Just as it is wrong to press the Gospel on those who have not been prepared by God, it is equally wrong to withhold the Gospel from those who have been taught by God, who are broken in spirit, and who are hungry for the mercy and forgiveness of the Savior.

Undoubtedly, some people will come to understand and will be well-prepared by the Holy Spirit to receive the Gospel before the teaching of the Gospels is to begin. When I was faced with this situation, I took the individual aside from the group and questioned him carefully to see if he clearly understood the basic truths concerning God, His holiness, hatred and judgment on sin, and the person's own sinful condition in God's sight. I first tried to determine if the person was truly convinced of his sinfulness and inability to save himself and if he understood and accepted God's Word. I then briefly, but carefully, told him of God's complete provision for sinners through the holy birth, life, sacrificial death, burial and victorious resurrection of Christ. If a person is truly prepared by God, faith in Christ will surely be the result of hearing and understanding the Gospel (John 6:44-45).

A young Palawano man named Kamlon was attending meetings where I had been teaching the Scriptures chronologically for about three months. One day, Kamlon came to me and said, "I am going to begin praying to your God." I had not prayed with the Palawano people during our teaching periods, but they knew the Roman Catholics prayed, and they had seen us giving thanks for our meals in our home.

I asked, "Kamlon, do you think that by praying you will be able to reach God? Don't you remember how God put Adam and Eve out of the garden and put His cherubim there with the flaming sword? Could praying remove the flaming sword? Could talking to God get them back into the garden?"

He answered, "No, it couldn't."

I asked, "Then why do you think that by praying you will be able to come to God? What is the punishment for sin?"

He replied, "Death."

We had already reached the story of the giving of the Law in our group meeting. So we talked together about the Old Testament stories which illustrate that death is God's righteous judgment on sin.

I said, "God requires death. It is a fixed price." This term, "fixed price," had been used during our teaching and is the term used in the Philippines when vendors indicate that they will not bargain for an article. In some larger stores, when a person begins to bargain, the sales assistant will often say, "Sorry, fixed price." They won't bargain because all the articles are at a fixed price. So I said to Kamlon, "God's price is fixed. God requires death. Prayer is not the price God requires. He will accept nothing less than death, which is separation from God."

Kamlon continued to attend the daily times of teaching; but, about one week later, he again came to speak to me. "Kalang Kayu," he addressed me. (This name, meaning Big Tree, was the name given to me by the tribal people because of my height in comparison to theirs.) "I realize now," Kamlon said, "that praying will not get me back to God. But, what am I going to do? I know from God's Word that I am a sinner. I am sure of that. I know that I am going to Hell. What can I do?"

Praising God in my heart for what the Holy Spirit had taught this man, I replied, "Kamlon, you have asked me what you can do. Tell me, what is the price to be paid?"

He answered, "Death."

I said, "Kamlon, if you want to pay for your own sin, then you must go to Hell. You will be separated from God forever. The punishment for your sin will never end."

He stood there looking thoroughly miserable and finally said, "Then I will have to go to Hell."

Immediately, I thought, "No, you won't." I knew that Kamlon had been taught by God. Through the Old Testament Scriptures, he had seen the basic truths about God, himself, and his sin. He was prepared to understand the Gospel and to trust in Christ alone for salvation.

"Kamlon," I said, "Come up and we will sit on the veranda." We went up and sat down. Then I questioned him, "Do you remember how that in the garden, after man sinned, God promised to send One who would be the child of a virgin? God promised that He would destroy Satan because he had brought man under his control."

He answered, "Yes, I remember."

I then reminded him of the story of Abraham. I asked, "Do you remember how God promised the Savior through Abraham?"

He replied, "Yes, I remember that."

I went over the key Old Testament stories which point forward to the coming Savior. Then, on the basis of these Old Testament stories and God's promises concerning Christ, I said, "Kamlon, the Savior has already come."

During the next hour or so, I briefly told him the story of Christ. When I finally came to the point where Christ died in our place, I told Kamlon, "God knew you would be born. God knew you would be a sinner. God knew you would deserve everlasting punishment because of your sinfulness. And God knew He could not save you unless that debt of sin was completely paid. The Lord Jesus, because of His great love, agreed to come and take the responsibility of paying for all of your sin."

When I spoke of Christ's death on the cross, Kamlon said with a great big smile on his face, "Then if He died for me, I don't have to die. He is my debt-payer."

Right there and then, his soul rested in the truth of the Scriptures. He trusted in Christ as his debt-payer. He accepted the fact that what he could not do, God had done for him.

Dennis and Jeanie O'Keefe who are missionaries to the Molbog tribe in Southern Philippines wrote the following about a young tribal man to whom Dennis taught the Scriptures chronologically.

"Almost every day, either coming or going to his rice fields, Saya would stop by my office for a cup of coffee, and we would talk. Precious were those times. He was beginning to understand real biblical truth. Present in his conversation was an awakening realization that he could not meet God's requirements and would be punished eternally for his sins and his sin nature.

"After I had taught in other villages, it was time to continue with Saya. So, in one day, Saya and I went from the tabernacle to the Cross. What a joy! All the pieces of the puzzle came together in the man Christ Jesus. He was stunned. As his mind raced from Genesis 3:15 to John 19:30, '... It is finished ...,' we sat in silence for a few moments. Then he said, 'Do you mean to say that He carried on Himself my sins?'

"God has done this, and it is beautiful in our sight. All of us can rejoice in the new horizons which have been made possible by God's grace demonstrated in this one man."

Brief encounters

I trust it is obvious all the way through this book that I have in mind situations where people can be taught over an extended period of time. This is possible in well-programmed missionary work, Sunday schools, Bible classes, and the ministry of the local church. But what does one do when he only has a short time to preach to people?

While we should never be bound to any teaching outline, we should always be guided, even in brief encounters, by biblical principles. One clear principle which we have already discussed is that only those prepared and drawn by God the Holy Spirit can and will come to Christ. God does not do what He commands us not to do. He does not throw pearls before swine.

We should not press the Gospel on unprepared people. But there is a great difference between the general public declaration of God's historical work in Christ for the whole world and the personal application of that work to an individual. A preacher in a public gathering, speaking to a mixed group of people whose hearts' condition he does not and cannot know, may have complete liberty to present the Gospel and all of God's gracious invitations to repentant sinners. Even so, he should always be aware that only those taught, convicted, and broken by God through His Word and the work of the Holy Spirit, will believe and appropriate the saving message of the Gospel. Those who reject the foundations of the Gospel – that is, the holy and righteous, but merciful character of God, and the sinful, lost and helpless condition of every man outside of Christ – cannot trust in the saving historical work of God the Son and be born of the Spirit. Therefore, even in public Gospel meetings where the speaker may not have the opportunity to teach the same people again, before God's good news of the Gospel is offered, the preacher should emphasize the nature and character of God and the demands of the holy and righteous Law of God.

In the book of Acts, when Paul entered a Jewish synagogue, he first reminded his hearers of the Old Testament foundational history wherein God revealed Himself and His promises regarding the coming Redeemer. Having done this, Paul then presented the claims of Jesus of Nazareth to be the long-promised Messiah, and showed that Christ's death and resurrection authenticated Him as God's appointed Savior for all who believe. Immediately, there was a division between Paul's hearers. The prepared ones longed to hear more; the hard-hearted and self-dependent rejected his message. Those who responded were taken aside and taught further by the Apostle, so that their faith would rest on a clear exposition of Old Testament Scriptures in the light of the new revelation in Christ.

In some situations, Christians have only a brief opportunity to witness to an individual – on a train, a bus, a plane, in a store, on the street, or at their home. The same biblical principles should be followed as much as possible, in spite of the limited time available. Rather than having a hit and run ministry in brief encounters, Christians should try to keep in contact with people and follow up with continued teaching, preferably in a Bible study. If that is impossible, then good

literature may be used which will lead them through the Scriptures and bring them to a clear knowledge of Christ.

In one area where we worked as missionaries in Palawan, the local witch doctor was an elderly woman. Her husband was gravely ill and no longer able to walk. Day and night, he lay on his sleeping mat.

I passed their house daily on my way to teach a leper who was the brother of the witch doctor. In the beginning, I stopped to greet them, to inquire about the man's health, and to ask if we could be of any assistance. At first, they resisted our offers to give them medical help, but after some time, they relented. Following this, I took the opportunity to stay for a while to introduce the Bible as the Word of God and to speak of God, the only eternal supreme being. Very soon after this, they sent a message through their grandson saying that they did not want to hear anymore about God. Following this incident, they could barely bring themselves to bid me the time of day. Their antagonism to us and our message was obvious in their whole demeanor.

The Palawano custom for a married man requires him to leave his own locality and live with his wife in her home area. But if he becomes very ill or knows that he does not have long to live, he will generally ask to be taken back to his own people. When the witch doctor's husband realized his death was imminent, he was carried back to the home of his relatives.

Sometime later, we were greatly surprised when some of his relatives walked three hours to request me to come and tell the dying man about God. This invitation was certainly evidence of God's work in his life.

Rejoicing in the possibility that maybe the little seed previously sown in his mind had been used by the Holy Spirit, I went immediately with his relatives to the house where he was. He was close to death, but he was still able to whisper brief responses to my few questions.

Sitting close by his side, I leaned over him and began to explain, "What I am about to tell you are not my words or the thoughts of people, but the words of the only true and living God."

Inwardly, I have never felt more helpless than I did that day. I was calling on the Lord to give me wisdom and clarity and to give the dying man understanding, conviction, repentance and faith.

I continued, "God tells us in His book that He created all things." I elaborated on this, adding, "God also created the first man, Adam, who was the father of the entire human race." I wanted this man to understand that this included the Palawanos and therefore him.

The old man appeared to be listening as I continued, "God placed Adam in a beautiful garden. In this garden, God had planted two very important trees, the Tree of Life and the Tree of the Knowledge of Good and Evil." After explaining in very simple terms the meaning of these two trees, I said, "God warned Adam that disobedience would bring death. Death not only means physical death but also everlasting separation from God in a place of punishment."

At this point, I suggested that he rest and think about what I had said. This also gave me an opportunity to teach his relatives who had gathered in the house.

Returning to him after a short while, I asked if he understood what I had told him so far. He assured me that he did, so from Genesis 3, I told of the temptation and fall of man. I then explained Genesis 3:15, "God promised that one day He would send a Savior who would destroy Satan and deliver man from his power. God put Adam and Eve out of the garden. They were shut out, away from God, without any way to return, unless God Himself made a way for them."

I then related the story of Cain and Abel to this old man. I emphasized, "Both Cain and Abel were born outside of the garden and were sinners because of their father, Adam. They were separated from God and could not escape the judgment of God against them for their sins, unless God Himself did something to save them."

The old man moved his position slightly in order to catch every word. I went on. "These truths apply to all people, and what is most important, they also apply to you. Because you, too, are a descendent of Adam, you were born away from God, cut off from the Tree of Life."

I paused and then explained how God instructed man that, if he wished to approach God, he must take a lamb and kill it. I stressed, "They had to come to God in the way which God had instructed them. They had to kill the lamb. Its blood had to be shed. Now, the blood of the animal could not pay for sin. But the blood had to be shed to remind the ones who offered the sacrifice that they deserved to die and that only God could save them. Their faith had to be in God, not in themselves or anything that they could do."

Then I briefly told the story of how Cain refused to come God's way and was therefore rejected, whereas Abel came God's way, trusting in God's mercy and promises and was accepted by Him. Having laid this groundwork, I applied all of these truths personally to my hearer.

"There is no way you can save yourself. Your sin must be paid for by everlasting separation from God. He will not accept anything less. Only God can save you. Like Abel, you must accept God's way if you want to be saved.

"Be warned. Don't be like Cain and think that you can come to God in your own way."

The old man looked thoughtful, and I said, "I will let you think about what you have heard, and then I will tell you what God has done so that you can be forgiven of all your sins and be saved from the punishment you deserve."

Returning a short while later to his side, I asked him a few questions, and he acknowledged, "Yes, I am a sinner." He then requested, "Tell me what God has done for me."

My heart was filled with joy as I unfolded, in the most uncomplicated way I could, the story of the Gospel.

"God sent His only Son into the world to be your Savior. Christ was born of the virgin, just as God promised. He lived a perfect life. The majority of people rejected Him and crucified Him. He could have destroyed them all and returned to Heaven, but He allowed them to nail Him to the cross so that He could pay the punishment for all the sins of mankind."

I reminded this old man who was so close to eternal damnation, "God's punishment for sin is everlasting separation from Him in terrible punishment."

Then I said, "When Jesus was dying on the cross, He called out, 'My God, my God, why have You forsaken Me?' Why do you think the Lord Jesus was forsaken by God? The Lord Jesus was forsaken and died to be the Savior of sinners. The Lord Jesus died for you to take your separation so that God could forgive all your sins and give you everlasting life."

I quoted John 3:16 and shared with him the story of the resurrection.

Sitting close by his side and looking into his face which already had death etched on it, I told him, "The Lord Jesus can see you right now, just where you are lying on your sleeping mat. If you trust in Him and accept His payment on the cross for your sin, God will forgive you for all your sins."

There was a note of urgency in my voice as I continued, "If you accept him, you will not go to the place of everlasting punishment, but to Heaven to be with God forever.

"Don't be like Cain," I implored him. "Don't think that you can come to God in your own way. Your sin has to be paid for, and there is only one payment that God will accept; that is, the payment the Lord Jesus Christ made for you when He was forsaken by God because of your sins.

"Do you understand? Do you want to ask me any questions?" I inquired.

With barely a whisper, he answered, "Yes, I understand." He seemed to be deep in thought as he closed his eyes.

Hiking back through the jungle to our own home in the gathering darkness, my heart was calling on the Lord in His great mercy to save that man.

A short time later, we were visited by some of this old man's relatives who told us that the man had died in the early hours of the morning after my visit. But before he died, he had told them to tell the Big Tree (my tribal name) that there was no need to worry about him because he was trusting in the Lord Jesus who had taken the punishment for his sin. Praise God for His great mercy and the simplicity of the Gospel!

Situations vary greatly. Sometimes we may not have even as much time as I had with this dying man. We should do whatever we can in the time given to us by the Lord to make the Word of God clear and plain and trust the Lord to use whatever we are able to say in brief encounters. But whenever possible, it is our responsibility to teach in such a way so that people will know why they must come to Christ and so that they will trust only in Him and His death on their behalf.

Evangelism for mixed groups – unbelievers and believers

Many groups and churches, like those which we first taught in Palawan, are confused regarding the way of salvation. The *Firm Foundations* curriculum has been effectively used to teach such churches and groups. Many individuals, who previously thought they were children of God, have been enlightened to their true condition through the Old Testament revelation of God's holiness, His demands for perfection as revealed through the Law, and His terrible judgments on rebellious sinners. Then, through the story of the Gospels, they have seen for the first time that they have no need to work for their salvation, for Christ has provided all that God righteously requires.

I wish I had understood this when I first began to teach the tribal churches in Palawan. I tried to straighten out their understanding by first teaching justification topically and then expositionally from the Epistle to the Romans, even though they did not have solid Old Testament foundations. In spite of the difficulties I faced in teaching and they faced in understanding, many Palawano church members were eventually enlightened to their lost condition and came to trust in Christ. But how much more simple and clear the teaching and learning process would have been if I had followed the divinely revealed order and taught chronologically through the Old Testament as preparation for the Gospel of grace revealed in the New Testament!

Years later, after I had seen my mistakes and had taught the Scriptures chronologically in another area of Palawan, I returned to the area of our initial labors to teach chronologically from Genesis to the ascension of Christ. After teaching them for a short time, some of the elders came to me and asked, "Why didn't you teach us this way from the beginning? This way of teaching makes everything so much clearer!" They could now see how everything they had been taught previously from the New Testament fit together with the Old Testament and was one comprehensive whole. I readily agreed with them, because it was also obvious to me that those whom I had taught chronologically from the beginning had a clarity of understanding of the Scriptures and the Gospel far beyond those taught only topically or expositionally from the New Testament.

The following material was written by Tim Cain and Larry Richardson, concerning the Puinave Indian work in Colombia.

"When we went into the Puinave work, we went with the assumption that there was a legitimate New Testament Church which lacked good teaching. But the more we understood of the language and the people, the more we realized there were some real problems. We came to the conclusion that the majority of the Puinaves who called themselves 'Christians' were, in fact, spiritually dead. Here are some of the things that we observed:

A) The 'elders' tried to force the younger generation to conform to 'Christianity.' Christianity to them meant (l) no smoking or drinking, (2) going to meetings daily, (3) going to conference, (4) giving a testimony by confessing a few sins or promising to live without sin from now on, and (5) getting baptized.

B) The people did not have an in-depth understanding of the Word of God. They knew a few Old Testament stories and a bit more from the New Testament, but they had no idea of the chronology of the stories or their significance.

C) There was no spiritual growth.

D) The people continued to practice witchcraft. The witch doctor was condemned, but his methods were not.

E) Genuine conviction of sin was not apparent.

F) The death of Jesus seemed to be something additional that God deemed necessary.

"We began to step back in our minds, trying to find where we should start teaching, and we found ourselves back at the beginning. The chronological approach was of great inspiration and help to us.

"As I (Tim) began to teach, I apologized to them for the confusion we had caused by not beginning at the beginning, and I promised that I would try my best to do it right this time.

"We taught up to the ascension of Christ, and all along, the people showed great interest. But nothing happened.

"What do you do but go over it all again?

"On the third time through, they began to spontaneously voice their understanding and acceptance.

"Alberto, one of the village leaders, told me he had come very close to going to Hell. He said he had 'played church' for 30 years and that his baptism was 'just a bath.' But now, he understood that it wasn't what he had done but what Jesus had done for him that made him right with God.

"One very old tribal man stood up at the end of one of our teaching sessions to testify. Standing there in all that noise and confusion, he said, 'I finally understand. I am a very bad sinner, but Jesus paid the price for my sin with his death.' The people around him tried to get him to sit down but he said, 'No, I want to say this!' He went on to share a clear testimony.

"Another man, who is a deacon in one of the Puinave churches, also testified, 'Up until now, I have always thought that God would accept me because of the things I have done for Him. I was baptized. I helped call the people together for meetings. I always got lots of food together so we could receive the people well when we hosted conferences. I always participated in the pre-dawn prayer meeting. I'm sure those are the things God saw upon my heart, because they are the things I was offering to Him in order to be able to approach Him. But now I understand that those things are just like the fruits Cain offered God, so I have removed them and replaced them with the blood of Christ. That's what God sees now upon my heart. That is what I am

offering to God now, just like Abel slew the animal long ago.'

"In another Indian conference, we were also teaching from the first part of the Bible chronology. Alberto, who had been a believer for a year or so at the time, was helping teach, and he was also translating into Curipaco for those who did not understand Puinave. He and I both felt this particular group was not yet ready to apply what we had been teaching to salvation. Therefore, we closed the last meeting simply with an exhortation for the listeners to think carefully about what they had heard and to ask themselves what it was that they might be offering to God. Suddenly, without my even noticing it, an old lady stood up way back in the shadows and began to speak in Curipaco. In a moment, I became aware that something was going on and waited for an explanation. It was soon forthcoming. Alberto turned and told me, 'That old lady says she has found her offering – the blood of Jesus Christ, which He shed on the cross. That's what she will offer to God.'

"These people had previously received topical teaching from other missionaries and had read from the New Testament for many years, so this was not by any means their first exposure to Christianity."

Many churches throughout the world are a mixture of saved and unsaved. People who attend church are at different stages in their spiritual experience. This has been evident to me in the churches in Australia where I have served as pastor. Some church members are saved but lack assurance of their position in Christ. Others are not saved but are convinced that they are. After many years of church attendance, many believers lack understanding of the history and chronology of the Old Testament and so lack the background for understanding much of the New Testament.

What is the answer? Exposition of God's Word chronologically! Many who have taught the *Firm Foundations: Creation to Christ* lessons to mixed groups – saved and unsaved – have testified to the great benefit their hearers have experienced regardless of what stage they were at in their spiritual understanding. Correctly teaching and expounding the Old Testament stories has strengthened believers in their understanding of Old Testament history, their appreciation of the nature and character of God, and has given them a fresh insight into their own unworthiness and a greater appreciation of God's mercy and grace in Christ. Many who were unsure of their salvation or deluded regarding their position before God have come to a firm and settled faith in all Christ has done for them to meet all God's righteous demands.

7

Correct Foundations for Teaching Believers

This book thus far has emphasized biblical guidelines for evangelism. At this point, I would like to turn our attention to biblical principles for teaching believers.

When I was teaching among the Palawano, monthly Bible conferences were of prime importance in my teaching program. Each month over one hundred elders and Bible teachers from the scattered Palawano churches would gather to be taught. These conferences were aimed at establishing the leaders and, through them, their churches in a basic understanding of the complete revelation of the Scriptures.

Because I had been schooled in traditional Bible teaching methods, the majority of my early teaching ministry at these monthly Bible conferences was done topically. I would teach on topics based on many different verses throughout the Bible.

It became evident to me from the practical difficulties I encountered that topical teaching was not the best form of Bible teaching for these Palawano conferences. Why? One factor was that topical teaching demands a high level of literacy, and these church leaders were poorly-educated. In addition, topical teaching uses verses from many locations in Scripture, but these church leaders were not well conversant with the location of the individual books in the Bible. And of primary concern, these Palawano church leaders lacked a basic understanding of the overall progressive and historical biblical revelation.

Many of these practical difficulties were accentuated due to the poorly-educated people whom I was teaching. However, **the major problems I found with topical teaching are equally relevant whether one is teaching poorly-educated or well-educated people.**

In this chapter, I will first share some of my experiences with tribal believers which impelled me to look to the Scriptures for a more logical and practical method of teaching them the Word of God. After pointing out the problems perpetuated by an over-emphasis on topical teaching, I will show from the Scriptures that progressive revelation is fundamental when teaching believers. If we are to successfully teach biblical topics, believers should first be taught progressively through the Old and New Testaments.

Topical teaching is difficult to follow.

The men who attended the Bible conferences were mostly poorly-educated and inexperienced in the Scriptures. They wasted much time as they searched for the numerous references necessary to establish the doctrine being taught.

When I gave a Scripture reference, there would immediately be a great deal of mumbling and whispering. They could not easily remember the reference given, so they were continually inquiring what the reference was from whoever was sitting near them.

When the first ones to find the verse located it, they would often begin reading the section audibly, laboriously sounding out letters and words.

Instead of paying attention to my teaching, they were absorbed in inquiring from one another what the reference was or trying to find the verse or trying to read the passage which they were so pleased to have found. Instead of their minds being occupied with the subject being taught, they were repeatedly distracted because they had to find the portions from many parts of the Bible.

Difficult to record, review, and reteach

After attending the monthly Bible conference, the Bible teachers were to go back to their congregations and teach them the same truths they had learned during the conference. In order for them to teach their congregations, these Bible teachers needed to have a way to review what they learned. In order to review the subject matter, they needed to write down all the references and make notes regarding which part of the verse had to be emphasized.

The church leaders' attempts at taking notes were usually terrible. The notes they made were of little use for review and too sketchy for them to use as a guide in teaching others. The notebooks which I provided for them were soon dirty and tattered and falling to pieces, especially after being tucked up between the palm-leaf roofing in their huts.

Nevertheless, they struggled to do their best to take notes. They wrote down each reference, carefully and painstakingly forming the letters and figures with a stub of a pencil or their modern bull-pin, as they called their ballpoint pens. Admittedly, after much practice, they did improve, and the younger men became quite proficient in note taking, but what an unnecessary and time-wasting exercise.

Eventually, I typed and duplicated simple notes for them. These were a great help, but they caused other problems as these men tried to reteach the outlines in their home churches. If only I had taught them the Scriptures expositionally in line with the way in which God revealed His Word! The teaching, learning, reviewing, and the passing on to others of that teaching would have been relatively easy for them to follow.

Difficult to focus on only one phrase in a verse

Often, in topical teaching, only a phrase or a few words from a verse are needed to establish the doctrinal point being taught. This is a difficult concept for many people to comprehend. It was certainly troublesome for the Palawanos who tend to view subjects as a whole rather than in separate parts. This particular problem came to my attention after I had prepared a book of doctrines to be taught in the churches. I would teach a topic from this book to the church leaders, and they would return to their churches and teach the same subject to their own village congregations.

During one conference with these men, I taught from this book of doctrines on the nature and character of God. The following weekend, according to my custom, I hiked to a tribal church to give on-the-spot teaching to the whole church and to check how the elders were handling the teaching which had been assigned to them. On Sunday morning, I listened as one of the tribal elders began to teach. He turned to the point in the outline, "God is love." Under this heading, various references were listed, one being John 3:16. The elder read this verse, and then he began to teach. First, he emphasized that God is love from the words, *"For God so loved the world."* According to the topical outline he had been given, that was as far as he was to go in John 3:16. But he continued. He went on to teach on the incarnation, basing his comments on the words, *"that He gave His only begotten Son."* And he didn't stop there. He continued reading, *"that whoever believes in Him should not perish,"* and he emphasized the necessity of faith in Christ and the perishing condition of those who do not believe. He finished reading *"but have everlasting life,"* and concluded his exposition of John 3:16 with comments on the certainty of everlasting life and the bliss of Heaven for all believers.

While he and his hearers were enjoying God's Word just as God had recorded it, I was frustrated and disappointed. I wanted him to teach as I had taught him at the conference from my book of topical, systematic theology. I wondered if they would ever be able to teach God's Word correctly. To teach it correctly, I reasoned, was to teach it analytically and topically.

As I sat there feeling I had failed and wondering what was the best way to train them to become able teachers of the Word, it suddenly occurred to me that the Holy Spirit wrote John 3:16 just the way the tribal elder had expounded it. Why then arrange it under subject headings? How much more straightforward and uncomplicated teaching and learning would be if all of the Scriptures were taught expositionally just as they have been revealed and recorded.

We make the teaching and learning of the Scriptures unnecessarily hard when we insist on topical teaching as our primary method of instruction. Western culture approaches most subjects analytically. We feel it necessary to dissect everything, examining and categorizing each portion. But many cultures do not approach the teaching and learning process in this way.

When the Lord prepared the Scriptures, He had all people in mind. If He had planned to speak only to us Westerners and had asked us what literary form His writing should take, our answer would probably have been, "A systematic theology." Wisely, the Lord did not do this. The Scriptures were not prepared in an analytical, topical form, for apparently this is not the preferable way to teach God's Word, even in Western culture.

While these things were going through my mind, the tribal elder proceeded to expound the next verse listed in the outline, and I began to observe the different people in the congregation. Across the aisle, a precious old lady who dearly loved the Word of God was holding her New Testament close to her face, trying to read it in the dim light. Other women were trying to follow the references and keep their attention on the speaker, in spite of the constant distractions caused by crying babies, wriggling and whispering children, and surly, growling dogs. The men and boys were all seated on my side of the palm-leaf and bamboo chapel. All ages were present. As I watched them, I wondered how much they really understood. Did they understand enough to be built up in true heart knowledge so their lives would reflect the character of the Lord? How much would they remember during the week? Would they be able to review the teaching in the quietness of their houses scattered through the jungle?

The Palawano believers were encouraged to pass God's message on to others during the week when they were working in their fields, washing clothes, pounding rice, visiting, or just sitting around the fire at night. I also wondered if they understood clearly enough to be able to do this.

As I looked at this congregation with all ages and differing reading and writing abilities, I realized that our complex teaching methods hinder the spread of the Word of God by the average person. We feel we have to arrange the Scriptures into individual topics and under, what we think, are suitable headings. How much simpler it would be if they were taught verse by verse and book by book! They would not need to turn to verses all over their Bibles or write down numerous references. At home, reviewing the section studied in the meeting would be greatly simplified. Discussing and sharing the portion with others would be much easier. Preparing for the coming meeting would be uncomplicated, for they would only have to read the next portion of Scripture instead of many scattered verses.

Large sections of the Scriptures overlooked

We all have a tendency to ride our own hobby-horse and gravitate to the subject or doctrines which we feel are most important. The result is that large sections of the Scriptures are usually overlooked, while other parts of the Bible receive most of the attention.

In Palawan, the tribal teachers taught the same topics and passages over and over. Rather than teach unfamiliar, unexplored sections of God's Word, they returned frequently to the same verses or topics.

Misinterpretation of verses out of context

Due to topical and doctrinal sermons on isolated Scripture portions, many who have been Christians for a long time are not able to interpret even familiar verses in the context of the book or epistle of which they are a part. The reason for this is obvious. It's because they seldom, if ever, have been taught the wider context of these well-known verses. Having never been introduced to the basic framework of biblical progressive revelation, they may understand verses, or even chapters or sections of Scripture which deal with some particular topic, but they do not understand the Bible as one book. They do not comprehend the great necessity to interpret all Scripture in the light of the whole of progressive revelation.

This was emphasized to me by the sermon of a sincere tribal man on Matthew 24:2, *"And Jesus said to them, 'Do you not see all these things? Assuredly, I say to you, not one stone shall be left here upon another, that shall not be thrown down.'"* After reading this verse, he pointed to the rocky hills surrounding the grass-roofed chapel where he was standing. He solemnly warned the people that when Jesus comes again to judge the world, all the stones on the hills around them would be cast down. "Not one will remain upon the other," he emphasized.

While I sat there trying to still my inner turmoil at his incorrect interpretation, the truth dawned on me that he was not to blame. I was to blame. I had led him to scattered verses when teaching a doctrine or developing a topic, but I had not consistently taught the Scriptures in such a way that he could understand the need to interpret verses in context or how to do it.

It was through such incidents that I was prompted to turn from using the topical teaching approach to the more simple and direct method of verse-by-verse exposition in order to help the people understand Scripture in its immediate context. But this, too, proved inadequate, for the believers had not been taught the Old Testament Scriptures which provide the background and foundation for the New Testament. They did not understand God's Word as one book.

God's teaching method

God's fundamental form of teaching throughout all history is clearly progressive. God gradually unfolded the Bible's message over the ages. This God-controlled unfolding of truth has been likened to the growth of grain, *"first the blade, then the head, after that the full grain in the head"* (Mark 4:28). God chose to make known His nature and character, His plan for the world, His purpose of redemption through Christ, and all other spiritual matters through progressive revelation.

God's basic method of teaching can be likened to the way an artist paints a picture. An artist does not begin painting in one corner of the canvas and immediately complete every detail. Instead, he will often do an initial, simple, light sketch of the whole picture. To an onlooker, the picture in the early stages will be indistinct. Even when studied, it may not be clear just what the artist intends to include in the final product. But, as the artist continues to work on the picture, here a little and there a little, the details begin to develop with greater clarity. This process continues until the final strokes are applied and the picture is complete.

This is how God painted His picture of the drama of redemption. He began the sketch in the early chapters of Genesis. Genesis 3:15 is a simple, undetailed sketch of the whole picture of the redemption story. Sharper, clearer details were then added by God in the call and life of Abraham. More color and features were put onto the canvas in the offering of Isaac and the perfect lamb substitute which God provided. Jacob's dream, the Passover, the manna from Heaven, the water from the smitten rock, the giving of the Law, the building of the Tabernacle, the brazen serpent, Joshua's victorious ministry, and other historical events are all strokes of the Artist's brush as He painted the background of the picture. The Master Painter continued adding details as He guided the events of Old Testament history toward the revelation of Christ, the main subject of the painting. Obscure images and lightly sketched areas suddenly emerged when Jesus came to live, die, and rise again. But even then, the canvas did not contain the whole picture. Through the apostles, the Holy Spirit continued the painting. The final strokes to God's picture were made when the revelation of Jesus Christ, given to John on the Isle of Patmos, was added.

God never taught all there was to know about any particular doctrine or subject at one specific time. He often revealed some new area of truth, but He never immediately gave the whole truth regarding any one subject.

God's method of teaching can be compared to the way most people prefer their meals served. A man would be surprised if he went home to find his wife had prepared a meal consisting only of potatoes and if he heard her say, "Today, we are having potatoes. Tomorrow, we will have beans. The day after tomorrow, we will have just meat on the menu." Who would be happy with that type of menu? We usually like a meal to consist of different types of vegetables and some meat. This is how God feeds us from His Word when we study it just as He has given it. Turn anywhere in God's Word, and you will readily see that one verse can give information, either directly or indirectly, about many different subjects. Whole books could be written by carefully examining and expounding one verse. Just as there are many facets on a diamond, a verse, when scrutinized under the guidance of the Holy Spirit, will reveal many different points of truth relating to many different doctrines.

During some seminars with missionaries, I have asked an individual to turn in the Bible to the doctrine of the Holy Spirit. I have requested that another turn to the doctrine of Man, another to the doctrine of Satan, and another to the doctrine of the Church. Some people have started to open their Bibles, and then hesitated. They could not turn to a specific doctrine, because the teaching of doctrines is not grouped together in the Bible. All doctrines begin in seed form in Genesis and are progressively revealed, little by little, throughout the Old and New Testaments. It is impossible to turn to a complete doctrine by turning to one place in the Bible.

Let's consider God's method of revelation and instruction in the life of every individual He prepared for His service during the history of the Old Testament. We see that He revealed truth and instructed each one in a clearly progressive manner. When God created Adam, it was God's desire and purpose that Adam should be taught to know Him, in all His sovereignty, majesty and glory. How then did God begin to teach Adam? What method did God use? Did He systematically and topically teach Adam all there was to know about Himself, Adam's Creator? No! How mundane and limited God's first revelation to Adam appears to be! God said, *"Be fruitful and multiply; fill the earth and subdue it; have dominion over the fish of the sea, over the birds of the air, and over every living thing that moves on the earth"* (Genesis 1:28). The Lord then told Adam what he and Eve were to eat. In this initial revelation, God did not even speak directly of Himself. Yet, by what He commanded, God revealed basic and important truths about Himself. By commanding Adam to be fruitful and to multiply, the Lord clearly declared Himself to be Adam's lawgiver and the master of every area of life. By authoritatively placing Adam as His vice-regent over the whole earth, and by commanding Adam to have dominion over every living thing in the earth, He was showing Adam that He, the Lord, is the rightful owner of the earth and all things in it.

After God had placed Adam in the Garden of Eden, He again spoke to him and at that time commanded him regarding the Tree of Life and the Tree of the Knowledge of Good and Evil. This was but a further revelation of God's role in His relationship to man. By the solemn declaration that death would be the inevitable punishment for disobedience, God was showing Adam that He alone is God, the judge and executor of righteousness in the earth. These are the only accounts that we have of the words of God to Adam before Adam's disobedience. But as God met with man, it would seem that He planned to teach Adam progressively, adding slowly to those initial revelations of His will and plan, according to Adam's ability to assimilate the information given to him.

How did God teach Abraham when He called him? Did God call Abraham and say, "Now, Abram, before you leave Chaldea, I want to tell you all My plans for you and your descendents?" No! Abraham went out, not knowing where the Lord was leading him. God revealed only what was necessary for each stage of Abraham's experience. Through progressive revelations, God taught Abraham, adding knowledge to knowledge, for Abraham was to walk by faith.

Further illustrations of God's progressive teaching method are evident in the stories of Jacob, Joseph, Moses, and the nation of Israel. Surely, even by these examples, it is obvious that God's basic way of teaching in the Old Testament was progressive – a slow, careful, building process.

The Lord Jesus Christ's teaching method

The Lord Jesus did not teach His disciples everything there was to be known about any one subject at one particular time. He taught His disciples progressively. Look, for example, at John 14. The Lord began comforting and encouraging His disciples (verse 1). He then spoke of His future ministry of preparing dwelling places for His children (verses 2-3). This was followed by a discussion with Thomas and Philip about the way to see and know the Father (verses 4-11). After this, He spoke of the need for obedience and the coming Holy Spirit (verses 12-17).

The Lord Jesus usually included many relative subjects in His discussions with the disciples, but He dealt with none exhaustively. Having introduced a subject or some aspect of a subject, He would then leave His disciples to think about it. Often, a question by the disciples would raise the subject again at a later date. If expedient, the Lord would then give His disciples more information; but even then, He would not tell them all there was to be learned and understood about the matter.

The Lord never gave out mere information. Rather, He presented transforming truth which needed to be understood and appropriated. Even at the close of His earthly life, He said, *"I still have many things to say to you, but you cannot bear them now. However, when He, the Spirit of truth, has come, He will guide you into all truth"* (John 16:12-13).

The Holy Spirit's teaching method

When the Holy Spirit came, how did He teach? Did He immediately reveal to the disciples all there was to be known about the New Testament Church and Christian living? Did He teach them topically and exhaustively on everything which God planned to reveal to the Church? No!

Again, it was progressive teaching, for God was continuing His usual form of revelation. It was a building process. Foundational truths, partially revealed or hidden in the Old Testament, and truths introduced by the Lord Jesus yet not fully revealed before His ascension, were slowly and carefully taught by adding knowledge to knowledge so the Church would be brought to *"the stature of the fullness of Christ"* (Ephesians 4:11-16).

The apostles' teaching method

Because God has revealed all truth progressively, the apostles based their teaching and writings on God's previous revelations in the Old Testament and His more recent revelations through His Son, the Lord Jesus. Their writings cannot stand alone, for they are the continuation and culmination of God's progressive revelation which He first initiated through Moses. All that the apostles wrote and taught was on the basis of the Old Testament.

The following portions from Paul's writings illustrate that the principle of progressive revelation continues on through Acts to the book of Revelation. Because of progressive revelation, it is impossible to clearly teach believers the New

Testament without first introducing them to the Old Testament.

Imagine a believer who has not been given Old Testament foundational teaching, trying to understand a portion such as 1 Corinthians 5:6-8, *"Your glorying is not good. Do you not know that a little leaven leavens the whole lump? Therefore purge out the old leaven, that you may be a new lump, since you truly are unleavened. For indeed Christ, our Passover, was sacrificed for us. Therefore let us keep the feast, not with old leaven, nor with the leaven of malice and wickedness, but with the unleavened bread of sincerity and truth."* How could anyone possibly understand these verses without the necessary Old Testament foundational knowledge?

In 2 Corinthians 3, Paul contrasted the ministry of death through Moses and the ministry of life brought by Christ. He said, *"unlike Moses, who put a veil over his face so that the children of Israel could not look steadily at the end of what was passing away. But their minds were blinded. For until this day the same veil remains unlifted in the reading of the Old Testament, because the veil is taken away in Christ"* (2 Corinthians 3:13-14). This whole chapter, and particularly these verses, cannot be understood except in the light of the Old Testament.

What about the Epistle to the Galatians? How could anyone understand Paul's arguments about law and grace apart from a proper foundation in the Old Testament? The churches in Galatia, through the influence of the Judaizers, had turned away from interpreting the Scriptures according to the historical order of progressive revelation. When combating this error, Paul reminded them of the sequence of historical events recorded in the Old Testament through which God progressively revealed the doctrine of justification. In Galatians 3, we are told that the Judaizers were emphasizing obedience to Moses and the Law as necessary for salvation. They were saying, "Yes, Christ's death is necessary for salvation, but believers must also keep the Law." How did Paul meet their arguments? Paul took his readers back into Old Testament history and showed that the doctrine of justification can only be understood according to progressive revelation. Paul wrote, *"And this I say, that the law, which was four hundred and thirty years later, cannot annul the covenant that was confirmed before by God in Christ, that it should make the promise of no effect. For if the inheritance is of the law, it is no longer of promise; but God gave it to Abraham by promise. What purpose then does the law serve? It was added because of transgressions"* (Galatians 3:17-19).

What was Paul doing? He was showing that the Law cannot supersede God's covenant of grace and faith as the way of justification, because grace and faith were revealed before the Law was given. Paul reminded the churches in Galatia of the order God used to progressively reveal these two doctrines. The Gospel was first preached to Abraham; and 430 years later, the Law was given through Moses to reveal sin as exceedingly sinful. The full revelation of the Gospel was finally given through Christ. This same Gospel was preached to Abraham. All believers are the children of Abraham by faith and are not dependent upon the keeping of the Law for salvation. Therefore, Paul made it clear that the sequence of historical events is vital in our interpretation and understanding of the Word of God.

Consider the doctrine of the Holy Spirit. In this present dispensation, we cannot appreciate what God has done for us through the indwelling of the Holy Spirit unless we first understand the work and ministry of the Holy Spirit in the Old Testament. The joy and liberty which are rightfully ours as part of the body of Christ are only experienced if we first understand that, during the old dispensation, the Holy Spirit was only **with** believers. Now He is **in** us. The doctrine of the Holy Spirit can only be comprehended on the basis of progressive revelation.

This is equally true of the doctrine of adoption. In Galatians 4, Paul taught that the Old Testament believers were like small children in the Father's household. Numerous laws and rituals controlled their every action. We, in contrast, have been placed into the family of God as adult sons. We share the Spirit of the Son, in contrast to the limited relationship which the Holy Spirit had with believers in the Old Testament. Our position through adoption can only be appreciated if we understand the historical and chronological development of God's relationship with believers as revealed in the Scriptures.

Consider Paul's letter to the Romans. As he introduced his main subject, the Gospel of God, he immediately reminded his readers that the Gospel was *"promised before through His prophets in the Holy Scriptures, concerning His Son Jesus Christ our Lord, who was born of the seed of David according to the flesh"* (Romans 1:2-3).

In Romans 1:18, Paul began to teach the doctrine of man's sin. He did this on the basis of the beginnings of history when the true knowledge of God was common to all men (Genesis 1-11). From this original revelation, Paul affirmed that man deliberately turned to gross idolatry and moral perversion.

In Romans 2, Paul proved the total depravity of all mankind by referring to the Law given to Israel at Mount Sinai and written in the hearts of the Gentiles.

In Romans 3, Paul quoted extensively from the Old Testament and then pointed to what the Law said as the final proof that all the world is guilty before God (Romans 3:19). He then maintained that the doctrine of justification which he taught was the same message to which the Law and the Prophets witnessed (Romans 3:21).

In Romans 4, Paul sited Abraham and David as examples of two sinners who were justified by faith.

In Romans 5, Paul laid the foundation for the doctrine of identification with Christ. Again, he pointed back to the Old Testament and showed that in Adam all sinned and all died. Death reigned as king over all because of the disobedience of the father and federal head of the human race. With these foundations, he then taught that Jesus Christ our Lord was prefigured in Adam and that He is the second Man. Just as Adam represented us as the federal head of the human race, so Christ was appointed by God as the new beginning, the federal Head of sinners, whom He represented by complete obedience to His Father, both in life and in death. Paul did not try to teach this liberating truth of the believer's complete identification with Christ apart from its Old Testament foundations.

If Paul taught Old Testament foundations when teaching believers, why should we think we can teach believers successfully without first laying the substructure on which all New Testament doctrines rest? It is impossible to clearly and correctly teach the New Testament to believers without adequate Old Testament foundations.

God's progressive revelation

The best way to teach God's Word is to follow His progressive form of revelation. We should first lay good foundations for the believer's faith and then build truth on truth, knowledge on knowledge. Bible doctrines can be most clearly understood if they are first seen in their beginnings in Genesis, then traced through the Old Testament historical accounts in which they were progressively developed, and then finally taught in their fullness in the New Testament.

God's progressive revelation of all truth has also been in conjunction with His historical acts in both Old and New Testaments. Therefore, all doctrines have an historical setting. New Testament doctrines are woven into the historical story of the Scriptures. The worldwide tendency is to teach Christians the doctrines of the Bible,

divorced from their God-given progressive and historical setting. This has resulted in doctrinal confusion in many sections of the Church. This is most clearly seen in the rapid growth of the Charismatic Movement, where doctrine is interpreted by personal experience, rather than according to its historical setting. The majority of doctrinal misinterpretations are due to failure to understand the historical, progressive revelation of truth in the Bible. Because so many endeavor to teach Bible doctrines almost exclusively from the New Testament, bypassing their beginnings in the Old Testament, many believers have a clouded and imbalanced interpretation of Bible doctrines. Doctrines can only be clearly understood in the light of their historical revelation and development.

Foundations for the topical approach

Western culture and education use an analytical approach to almost every subject. Since most subjects are treated in this way, it seems to be automatically accepted by Christians that if one really wants to know his Bible, he must analyze and categorize every part of the Word of God.

While there is a definite need for analysis in our study, the first and greater need is for a holistic approach to God's Word. This method of studying and teaching the Scriptures holistically has been called the synthetical approach, in order to distinguish it from the analytical method. The synthetic begins with the general and looks at the whole rather than individual parts. Analysis begins with the specific and then moves to the general.

Imagine trying to instruct a primitive tribal man in watchmaking and repairing. If he had never seen a watch nor understood its function as one instrument, he would find it impossible to understand the position and purpose of each separate part. The wisest procedure would be to first show him a complete watch. Following this, we could point out the minute parts and explain their individual contribution to the whole. This, too, is how we should approach and teach the Scriptures. The general, panoramic view provides the foundation for a more specific, analytical investigation.

The need for this holistic teaching of the Scriptures, before topical teaching is given, is clearly demonstrated by the experience of a missionary friend planning to go to the Philippines. When he returned to his home church to prepare his gear and await the time of departure, his pastor asked him to teach an adult Bible study. He decided to begin in Genesis and teach an overview of the Old Testament, leading into the New Testament. Later, when he met me in Manila, he said, "The more I taught, the greater the excitement and enthusiasm of my class. Even though these people had attended our church for many years, in all that time, they had never been taught the Scriptures chronologically and panoramically. At the close of one of the lessons, a lady asked, 'Why hasn't our pastor taught us like this? I have been hearing sermons all of my life but only now am I beginning to understand the Bible as one book!'"

New Christians usually struggle for many years with a vague understanding of the Scriptures as one book. The majority of preachers seldom, if ever, teach historically and chronologically through the entire Bible. Sermons on individual texts and topics, and even expositional teaching of passages of Scriptures and individual books, limit one's understanding of the Word of God to certain sections and scattered verses. Through a panoramic study of the Old and New Testaments, however, the Bible can be seen as one volume.

Teaching Bible topics should have an important place in our program, but it should be used only with those who have already been taught the Scriptures as a whole. If this is our normal approach, then topical teaching, when needed, will be far more effective. The truths we emphasize through topical teaching will be clearly understood and appreciated in the context of the whole of God's revelation.

Topical teaching in the Word of God is usually remedial. This is clearly evident in the ministry of the prophets whom God raised up to remind Israel of the righteous and holy laws which had been given to them in orderly progression through the ministry of Moses. The major part of the prophetic teachings is taken up with the topic of Israel's and Judah's rebellion and the warnings of God's coming judgments unless they returned in true heart repentance and obedience to the body of revelation already in their possession. The topical, remedial writings of the prophets are really interruptions in the straight line of God's progressive revelations pointing forward to Christ, the coming King and His kingdom.

Topical teaching then should be used when there is misinterpretation or disobedience to the Scriptures, or when there is a need to emphasize or clarify some particular doctrine.

Paul's letter to the Corinthians is another example of topical, corrective teaching. Paul is basically reminding the Corinthians of what he had already delivered to them as the body of revelation which they must believe and obey. His initial teaching to the Corinthians was the same as in every place. His teaching was based on the Old Testament Scriptures (Acts 18:4-5; 1 Corinthians 10:1, 11). To these, he added the teachings given by the Lord Jesus while He was here on earth (1 Corinthians 11:23). His instructions to them were then completed by adding the revelations which the Holy Spirit began on the day of Pentecost (1 Corinthians 2:1-13). It was from this complete body of revelation that Paul drew his corrective, topical teaching in an effort to remedy the situation in the church at Corinth.

Thus we see that corrective topical teaching is much clearer when it follows this basic pattern of progressive revelation. Because God has revealed all doctrines progressively, the simplest and clearest method to emphasize a particular doctrine is to trace its development from Genesis through to the Revelation. If, for example, the need is to teach on marriage, there is no better way than to begin in Genesis, just as Jesus did when He answered questions regarding marriage (Matthew 19:3-6). After reminding our hearers of God's original purpose for marriage, as shown in Genesis 2, we can then turn to other Scriptures on marriage in their chronological order. We could teach on Deuteronomy 24:1, where Moses permitted the rebellious Israelites to deviate from God's ideal standard for marriage, and then Matthew 19, where Jesus comments on this portion from Deuteronomy. Finally, we should teach the apostles' instructions relating to marriage from the Epistles, where God's original plan and standard for marriage are reaffirmed.

Imagine a church where the basic teaching method is to consistently teach God's Word as one complete book. The teachers methodically cover all the Word of God so that the congregation will continually advance in their understanding of the whole revelation of God in both Old and New Testaments. But problems are bound to arise at some time within the church; so, at these times, it will be necessary to digress from the usual teaching program and give topical, corrective teaching. If the Word of God has been taught consistently as one whole, it will be relatively simple to draw the necessary corrective topical teaching from many parts of Scripture. The Bible teacher will be able to say to those who have been taught the overall plan of Scripture, "Do you remember what we learned previously in 'such and such a Scripture' about this particular subject?" Because they have been taught the Scriptures holistically, the teacher will be able to draw from the entire Word of God as the authority for his topical, corrective teaching.

Foundations for expositional teaching

Thankfully there are concerned pastors and Bible teachers throughout the world who recognize the limitations and problems connected with topical teaching and sermonizing. Accordingly their usual form of teaching is expositional. This usually includes expounding passages of Scripture or the exposition of complete books, particularly New Testament books.

There is no doubt that this form of teaching is far superior to sermonizing or constant dependence on the topical approach. However, problems remain. One is that a great many preachers seem to teach with the assumption that their hearers have a similar knowledge of the Scriptures as they do. Through their studies, preachers often have been taught Bible history and have come to understand the individual contribution of each book of the Bible to the whole. In contrast, the average Christian usually has a very limited and fragmented understanding of individual books and the Bible as one volume. Therefore, unless believers are first taught the Bible chronologically, they will be unable to clearly understand the constant allusions and references from the Old Testament which will be encountered as they are taught the Scriptures expositionally. Nor will they be able to appreciate the contribution that the book being studied makes to the whole of Scripture.

Before teaching expositionally, pastors should first make sure that their congregations have been taught the Scriptures holistically. Only then should they feel confident that their hearers will be able to keep pace with them as they expound the Scriptures and quote verses from other books of the Bible. Through first being taught events and selected books expositionally to form an overview of God's Word, believers will have formed a framework in their minds of biblical history and have a basic understanding of the flow of progressive revelation. With this background knowledge, Christians are more suitably equipped to appreciate and understand verse-by-verse exposition of passages and complete books of the Bible.

Foundations for understanding the Law-and-Grace dilemma

Believers need to be taught the Old Testament so that they will be able to clearly distinguish the difference between the dispensation of Law and the dispensation of Grace. Old Testament foundations are necessary in order to understand the place of the Law during the Church age.

Believers will only be able to see the difference between Law and Grace if they are given a basic knowledge of Israel's position under the Law prior to the Cross. Legalism, which is prominent in many churches and devastating to the believer's faith and walk, can only be avoided by teaching progressively from the Old Testament into the New Testament. If there is a clear understanding of the purpose of Law in the Old Testament, there will be little danger of the misuse or misinterpretation of the Law in the New Testament. It will be obvious that no one was ever justified or sanctified by the Law and that believers are fully dependent on God's grace alone for salvation and the Christian walk.

Furthermore, unless the Old Testament history of Israel is first taught, it is difficult to understand the Jews' attitude toward the Gentiles at the time of Christ and the time of the early Church. Why were the Jewish leaders so angry at the suggestion of the Lord Jesus that the Gentiles could also be recipients of the grace and blessings of God? Why did the Church in Acts face such dilemmas regarding the matter of accepting uncircumcised believing Gentiles into full fellowship? Why was it necessary for the Lord to give Peter a special and thrice-repeated vision before he would take the Gospel into the home of a Gentile? Why was Paul hounded from city to city by the descendants

of Abraham? Why was it necessary for Paul to constantly address the topics of Jew and Gentile, Law and Grace, and circumcision and uncircumcision? The answers to these questions are found in Old Testament history.

Foundations for the Christian walk

Once people profess to be saved, most teachers are so zealous to see these new believers living and serving like Christians that they give them little time to grow in knowledge and experience. They are expected, in a very short period of time, to function like those who have been Christians for many years.

Just as the unsaved must be prepared for the Gospel of God's grace in salvation by a revelation of God's nature and character, so believers need to be prepared to walk humbly with the Lord by deeper insights into God's nature and character.

The truth of the verse, *"The fear of the LORD is the beginning of wisdom"* (Proverbs 9:10) should not only be applied to the unsaved but also to the believer and his growth in holiness. *"Oh, fear the LORD, you His saints! There is no want to those who fear Him"* (Psalm 34:9). The fear of the Lord in the life of the believer should not hold dread of condemnation or wrath, for there is *"no condemnation to those who are in Christ Jesus"* (Romans 8:1). However, through the knowledge of God in His holiness and glory as revealed in all the Scriptures, the Bible teacher should prepare foundations for the believer to respond to scriptural exhortations to godliness. The believer should continually advance in genuine awe and solemn appreciation of who and what God is. Only this will produce true biblical humility, brokenness of spirit, meekness and contriteness of heart. The fear of the Lord is the preparation for the life of holiness and obedience to which the believer is called.

The scriptural truths necessary for a victorious and holy walk can only be understood, appreciated, and correctly appropriated if seen and interpreted in light of God's glorious nature, character, and eternal purposes as revealed in all the Scriptures. The child of God must see God as the supreme reason for everything he does. The believer should respond to the scriptural exhortations to holiness out of love and worship of God. The biblical basis for the believer to pursue holiness is epitomized in the words, *"Be holy, for I am holy"* (1 Peter 1:16). The Apostle Paul says to believers, *"Therefore, whether you eat or drink, or whatever you do, do all to the glory of God"* (1 Corinthians 10:31). The foundation for worshipful service to God is a Bible-oriented appreciation of God's supremacy, majesty and holiness.

Believers need to come to know who God is before they are taught the things they must or must not do as believers. Anything less may produce counterfeit experiences which will lead people to glory in their own humility and dedication. Exhorting believers to holiness before they have these necessary foundations can easily lead them to mere outward conformity and perfunctory obedience based on the false foundations of human determination and fleshly dedication. Anything which the believer does for any reason other than genuine love and appreciation for who God is and what He has done is unacceptable to God, even when the believer's actions are based on some command from the Word of God.

Many sincere missionaries and Bible teachers lead believers into legalism because they fail to apply these biblical guidelines to their teaching methods. They immediately begin teaching new believers the dos and don'ts of the Christian life. They seem to think that, if they simply tell these new believers that because they are indwelt by the Holy Spirit, and stand on some particular positional truths, then this knowledge will bring the liberty and power to obey God's commands to holiness. Admittedly, these truths are vitally important and should be taught to believers, but the fact remains that spiritual growth is a process. Growth cannot be forced. It is the result of God's Word being understood and received in the heart. It is the result of God's Word dwelling in our lives (Colossians 3:16). The Word of God must be planted in the mind and heart in order for it to take root and grow (James 1:21). The growth of the believer comes not only through the knowledge of the written Word, but also through a deep and personal relationship with the Living Word – the Lord Jesus Christ (2 Peter 3:18). The believer must be *"rooted and built up in Him"* (Colossians 2:7).

The believer should grow spiritually through the teaching and appropriation of God's Word just as the human body develops and grows through eating and digesting good food (1 Peter 2:2; Ephesians 4:11-16). The human body develops slowly from infinitesimal beginnings. At birth, a child has all the potential of the adult, but there must be development and growth before the latent potentiality of the child can be exhibited. Forcibly overfeeding a child or immediately giving it the food of an adult will not promote growth but rather will inhibit its progress. What is true in the natural is equally applicable in the spiritual realm.

The faithful servant of God must be careful and patient, just as God has shown Himself to be patient while teaching and preparing men for His service. Let us not forget how long the Lord took to teach and prepare Abraham before He finally gave Abraham the promised son, Isaac, and even then, there was more training for the patriarch. We need to contemplate God's patient work in preparing Joseph in an Egyptian prison, Moses in the Midian desert, Joshua as a servant to Moses, David in the wilderness constantly hounded by Saul, John the Baptist in the wilderness, Jesus as a Nazarene carpenter's son for 30 years, the disciples' three years of training, and Paul's three years of training in Arabia. These are but a few examples of God's faithful, patient, slow work of teaching and preparing His most useful instruments. Since the divine Teacher feels it necessary to take time to instruct and allow His students to grow, we, too, need to take the time to see people well taught, not only in the New Testament but also in the Old Testament. *"For whatever things were written before were written for our learning, that we through the patience and comfort of the Scriptures might have hope"* (Romans 15:4).

When Paul taught the truths for the Christian walk, he did so on the basis of the Old Testament Scriptures. To the Corinthians he said, *"Moreover, brethren, I do not want you to be unaware that all our fathers were under the cloud, all passed through the sea"* (1 Corinthians 10:1). Paul did not want them to be ignorant of these Old Testament accounts. Why not? Because, he said, *"These things became our examples, to the intent that we should not lust after evil things as they also lusted ... Now all these things happened to them as examples, and they were written for our admonition, upon whom the ends of the ages have come"* (1 Corinthians 10:6, 11). Paul's presentation of God included God's historical revelations to the nation of Israel. Paul reminded Timothy that from a child he had known the Holy Scriptures, which, Paul assured Timothy, are able to make a person wise unto salvation through faith which is in Christ Jesus. Paul continued by saying, *"All Scripture is given by inspiration of God, and is profitable for doctrine, for reproof, for correction, for instruction in righteousness, that the man of God may be complete, thoroughly equipped for every good work"* (2 Timothy 3:16-17). It should be clear to all Bible teachers that Paul is speaking of the Old Testament Scriptures as well as the New Testament revelation.

What then is the best way to teach in order to give believers a knowledge of God as a basis for the Christian walk? We must teach all of the Scriptures according to the divinely provided pattern laid out in the Word of God. If we do not see and understand the teaching principles in the Scriptures, we will not be convinced of their importance to the spiritual development and growth of believers. The progressive, building approach to teaching will seem unnecessarily long and arduous. The quicker, more efficient way will seem to be, "Forget about the majority of the Old Testament and other introductory Scriptures. Just get on with the job and teach the Christian life." This attitude is akin to the one which says that the teaching of the Old Testament historical sections to unsaved people takes too long. In most cases, it is not the time factor which influences our thinking that way, but a lack in our understanding of scriptural teaching methods and our failure to appreciate the Lord's purpose for writing the Scriptures as He has.

Foundations for believers

There are many believers in churches who have not been taught the Scriptures holistically. Beginning from the time they were saved, these Christians have almost always been taught topically. Thus, their understanding of the Scriptures is fragmentary, for it is made up of isolated verses and portions of Scripture. They do not understand the Bible as one Book. In this type of situation, it is far more effective to begin by teaching the lessons in *Firm Foundations: Creation to Christ* (FFCC) and, on this sound basis, continue building scripturally. The Old Testament lessons should be taught, uninterpreted by the New Testament, so that believers will see and understand the progressive development of God's revelation.

Believers who have been taught the FFCC lessons, either as members of a mixed group of saved and unsaved or as a separate group of only believers, have greatly benefited by seeing the chronological and panoramic view of the history of redemption. Through it, they have been taught the basis of the faith and salvation of Old Testament saints. They have also received the Old Testament background necessary for a correct interpretation of the New Testament. The FFCC curriculum has also demonstrated to believers how to evangelize by first teaching the Old Testament lessons to convince people that they are hopeless and helpless sinners, rather than trying to persuade them that they need a Savior while they are still content in their sin or trusting in their own self-righteousness.

Don and Janet Schlatter, who ministered to the Lawa tribal people in Northern Thailand for many years, saw the Lord save a great number of the Lawa. The Schlatters taught these believers to function as members of indigenous church fellowships. After many years of teaching these believers, Don taught the Old Testament lessons to the Lawa churches. Don wrote,

> *"We praise God for the response in some of the older churches to the chronological presentation of Bible truth. We are going through the Old Testament passages which form a foundation to Christ's coming. One elder said it this way, 'Before, you taught us from the middle to the top of the tree. Now we are hearing about the bottom of the tree.' It brings into focus much which was confusing before. How we thank God for bringing this need to our attention. Lawa believers in 16 villages are now hearing the Word, and we are trying to present it in a logical fashion in every place."*

Mike Henderson, a missionary with the Aziana tribe in the highlands of Papua New Guinea, noted a change of emphasis in the ministry of the church elders and teachers, and a change in the type of teaching illustrations they used, after they had been taught the Old Testament lessons.

Prior to being taught the Old Testament, the Aziana tribal teachers limited their illustrations of God's judgment on sin to local experiences within the tribe. They did not know the Old Testament accounts of the revelation of the character of God, so when they wanted to give historical proof of

the scriptural picture of God, they looked for evidence and verification in the local happenings within the tribe. But local incidents, which initially appeared to the tribal people to be God's judgment on individuals, were dimmed through the passing of time. Different accounts and distortions of the incidents also undermined their usefulness as warnings to those who disregarded the Scriptures. All of this changed once the Aziana teachers had been taught the Old Testament. They were able to use illustrations of actual written historical happenings with the accompanying interpretation in the Scriptures. Their teaching of the New Testament became punctuated with Old Testament historical accounts of God's judgment and gracious provision, which could not be discounted nor changed. They were able to use the Old Testament writings for the purpose they were recorded by the Lord.

Foundations for future teachers

It is the responsibility of every Bible teacher to teach God's Word in such a way that the fellowship of believers will be able to interpret all doctrines in light of God's complete revelation. But does this mean that a Bible teacher or missionary who teaches believers in order to see them established as a New Testament church must teach every single verse of the Word of God, beginning in Genesis and concluding with the Revelation? No! That is not his responsibility.

The Bible teacher's primary responsibility is to lay the foundations. He should train and equip the local congregation and give them the responsibility to continue building on the foundations which he has laid down for them from the Word of God (1 Corinthians 3:10-15; Ephesians 4:11-13; 2 Timothy 2:2). The one who lays the foundations is responsible to make sure that the foundations he lays are wide enough to support all that must be taught later by the other teachers. If the foundations are inadequate and lacking in some way, then the teachers who follow will not have the necessary basis for teaching the whole counsel of God. The builder of the foundations must lay the theological, historical, dispensational, and doctrinal foundations which will support every part of God's revelation, so that the future local teachers will be able to correctly expound and interpret the entire revelation of God and all doctrines in both Old and New Testaments.

Which then is the simplest way to do this? Should we have doctrinal check lists and check the doctrines off as we teach them? No, because if we do, the future teachers will be as bound to our doctrinal outlines as they are to their Bibles. Rather, every ambassador for Jesus Christ should determine that, when teaching believers, he will be guided by the divine principles exemplified in the Word of God. By closely following these principles, the teacher will have done all in his power to bind his hearers' hearts and consciences to the complete Word of God and its glorious Author.

Be careful how you build

Paul reminded the Corinthian church, *"you are **God's** field, you are **God's** building."* He reminded the pastors and teachers that they, like Paul, were *"**God's** fellow workers"* (1 Corinthians 3:9).

Nothing has changed! The work of evangelism of the world and the building of the Church of Jesus Christ does not belong to some denomination or mission organization. The building of the Church is not our project. Jesus said, *"I will build My church, and the gates of Hades shall not prevail against it"* (Matthew 16:18).

Realizing the importance of this work of laying the foundations of Christ by evangelism, and then building on those foundations through the instruction of God's children, Paul solemnly warned all who would presume to be God's fellow workers. He said to be very careful how we build because *"the fire will test each one's work, of what sort it is"* (1 Corinthians 3:9-15).

God, the Architect and Master Builder of His Church, has provided His Word to be our greatest and most powerful tool as we prayerfully labor with Him. Paul was vitally aware of this as he spent his final days in a Roman prison. Knowing that his death was imminent, Paul wanted to leave final instructions for Timothy to whom he had entrusted his work. Paul wrote to Timothy, *"I charge you therefore before God and the Lord Jesus Christ, who will judge the living and the dead at His appearing and His kingdom: **Preach the word!**"* (2 Timothy 4:1-2).

What then will we do? We are now so very much closer to that *"glorious appearing of our great God and Savior Jesus Christ"* (Titus 2:13). Will we be found faithful workmen at His coming? Will our work stand the test of the all-seeing eyes of the risen Christ, the Judge? John said that the eyes of the glorified Christ were as *"a flame of fire"* (Revelation 1:14). In demonstration of His knowledge of all things, the Lord Jesus said to each of the seven churches in ancient Asia, *"I know your works"* (Revelation 2:1). What then will He say of our work done in His Name?

PART 2

How to Teach the Bible Chronologically

1

The FFCC Curriculum

These Bible lessons were designed to bring unbelievers to a saving knowledge of Jesus Christ. As you teach, you will be systematically building a solid foundation for your students to understand truths necessary for salvation.

The purpose of this course is to clearly present the nature and character of God and His message of salvation as He has progressively revealed these truths in the Bible.

Although many of the Bible passages in these lessons are rich in truths for believers, you will be teaching selectively, and not focusing on growth principles for Christians. Because this course is evangelistic, you should not advertise it as a "Bible Survey" or "Old Testament Survey." This is a foundational study, covering only those themes from Genesis to Christ that pertain to salvation.

Figure 1-1 is a suggested course description **in a church setting**.

Firm Foundations: Creation to Christ

This unique Bible study systematically lays a solid foundation for the Gospel. Those who have never heard or trusted in this wonderful story will learn what God did to provide our salvation. Those who already understand the Gospel will see God in a new and living way and come to understand how the Old and New Testaments fit together as one continuous story.

This curriculum's lessons follow God's pattern of progressively revealing Himself and His plan of redemption within the context of history. Beginning in Genesis and progressing through the Old Testament and the life of Christ, you will learn the key themes of the Bible and get to know the character of God. This study answers the most significant of all questions: "How can I be accepted by God?"

Figure 1-1

The target audience

Because these lessons are designed to teach truths necessary for salvation, obviously, the target audience is the unsaved.

But believers will benefit as well because they will gain a deeper knowledge of God and an understanding of the Bible as a whole, thus strengthening their faith.

Filling the Holes in Understanding

Jill had been a believer since she was a child and was well-acquainted with many biblical truths. But she loved getting the whole picture as we taught chronologically. It was a light-bulb moment the day she understood that the reason Jesus had to be born of a virgin was so that He would not inherit Adam's sin nature.

– Ruth

In addition to helping believers understand the Scriptures better, your teaching will be a pattern which they can follow in their own evangelistic outreach.

Getting to Know God

Eleanor, a lady in her 80's, sat under my husband's teaching in an adult Sunday school class. She was enthusiastic about what she was hearing and could be seen carefully taking notes. About three months into the sessions, she decided she wanted to teach this same curriculum in her home and invited 13 ladies.

"Paul's teaching was very helpful. I learned to emphasize God reaching out to man," she said. "At different points in the lessons, Paul always brought us back to the question 'What does this show us about God?'

"This is the way to teach others," she stated. "The end result is solid believers who have confidence in who God is."

– Pam

If your class includes believers, let them know from the beginning that you are going to concentrate on foundational truths. This will be addressed in Lesson 1 as you lay out the broad picture of how you are going to teach. You can also talk with believers privately and ask for their help in limiting the issues raised so that the unbelievers who come have the opportunity to gain a clear understanding of salvation by grace.

Stick to the themes presented in the lessons. Don't get sidetracked – either by your students or yourself – into teaching issues directed to believers, such as works, obedience and worship.

The focus – the Bible

God's Word is the authority and focus of this course.

The lessons are designed to be used by the teacher, along with the Bible. The students use only their Bibles; there is no "student lesson," although student notebooks are available.

Be certain that each student has a Bible available to him. If you supply Bibles for them, it would be preferable to choose ones without extensive study notes. If students are trying to read study notes while you are teaching, they can easily miss what you are saying, or become sidetracked by whatever is contained in the study notes.

Bible versions

Anytime Scripture is quoted in this curriculum, the version used is the New King James Version (NKJV). Should you decide to use another version, choose one that faithfully spells out the meaning of the original Scriptures.

Although it is not mandatory, it would be easier if all your students were to use the same version, because it makes it easier for them to follow along as Scripture is read.

Not an "instant" study

This curriculum is unlike traditional materials in that each lesson builds on the foundation laid in the previous lesson. For that reason it is extremely important that these lessons be taught consistently and thoroughly.

In a day of "instant everything," this is not an instant Bible study. You could easily and quickly acquaint a person with factual knowledge of the chronological order of the Bible. But these lessons are more than facts. They lay the foundational themes that prepare the student for salvation, based upon a true understanding of God as He has progressively revealed Himself in the Bible.

Building that foundation cannot be done overnight. It takes time for abstract spiritual concepts to be firmly grasped. Only clear teaching, done in the power of the Holy Spirit, can plant these truths firmly in the students' minds.

Misconceptions, too, are built over a lifetime. In addition to teaching truth, you will also be dismantling false teaching and mistaken beliefs which are already established in your students' thinking.

Corrective Teaching

In a perfect world no one would have misconceptions concerning God or the truths revealed in His Word. However, the "blinding" that Satan accomplishes in people is thorough and presents a real challenge to those of us who would be used of God to break down those strongholds. One merely needs to examine his own journey from false teaching and misconceptions to realize that this undoing-process takes time.

I have been teaching a men's home Bible study. A young man came; he was a new believer with very little grounding in the Word of God. Due to his chosen lifestyle as a teen and young adult, he was carrying a lot of "baggage" from his old life. When he began attending the study, it was obvious that he was confused on many basic issues. Rather than address those issues directly, or all at once, I assured him that as the teaching progressed, many of his questions would be answered.

At first it was uncomfortable holding some of his questions at bay so as to avoid following rabbit trails that would lead us away from the lesson at hand. And while the nature of his questions revealed huge misconceptions in regards to the person and character of God, and were very important questions to answer, it was just not productive to answer them all at once. I knew true convictions that make a difference in a life must be based on God's Word and not merely on a quick explanation about God's Word. When corrective teaching needs to be done, we must not give in to the temptation to look for shortcuts. It takes time! This young man needed to "see" God through personally being taught by Him before he could be convinced of who God really is and how biblical truths related to his daily living.

It has taken months for him to see how his previous misconceptions kept him in bondage and controlled him through unnecessary worries and baseless wrong attitudes towards God Himself. This young man's appreciation of God, through understanding His goodness, grace, faithfulness, etc., has grown exponentially. He also has an appropriate focus on his need of God and not on this messenger. This is the kind of maturity we all want to see produced in those we have been given to disciple, but we need to be willing to invest the amount of time it takes to see it happen.

– Earle

A one-year program

These lessons are designed to be used over a one-year period, either as a Sunday school curriculum or as a home or small-group Bible study which meets for an hour once a week. The schedule could be accelerated with more frequent or longer class sessions.

Is it worth this much time investment? Absolutely! People who go through this material – teachers and students alike – gain foundational understanding that helps them see the Bible as a whole. Their understanding of God and His Word become the basis for their lives.

Once the foundation is laid, all future understanding is built on that firm basis of truth. This invites continued personal Bible study because the pieces fall clearly into place. The impact on lives is immeasurable.

Worth Time and Effort

My neighbor became a believer at 87 in my home Bible study. I have taken him back through the lessons several more times because repetition helps, due to his age. Now, at 92, he states, "My life has become beautiful because I'm getting to know God. For 40 years I worked on bettering myself through a man-made program, but then you began to teach me from the Bible and I came to know Christ. I would not have had anything to live for if I hadn't become a Christian. I would have just wanted to die. I have changed, and now I talk to God every day and He helps me."

Before Frank became a believer, his wife had embraced the Truth. She penned this note to God in her journal, "I thank You for my missionary neighbors – that You have answered my prayers and my dear Frank is now reading the Bible and hearing and understanding Your truth. I am deeply grateful. Thank You for hearing me."

– Paul

2

Lesson Goals and Themes

Through the stories recorded in the Old and New Testaments, the Holy Spirit has emphasized many different doctrinal truths. Your responsibility is to teach and expound these Bible stories in such a way that each student will not only remember Bible history but that he will also come to a clear understanding, first of the nature and character of God, then of himself as God views him.

Lesson goals

These lessons are directed toward reaching primary goals. By the end of this curriculum, your students will, hopefully:

- Know the basic historical facts of the Old Testament and the Gospels
- See the wondrous nature and character of God revealed through His interaction with man in biblical history and through His Son, Jesus Christ
- Recognize that because of their sin they are separated from God
- Realize the impossibility of ever pleasing God by their own efforts
- Understand and believe that God has made a way for them to be restored to a right relationship with Himself through the Deliverer
- Trust in Jesus Christ as their personal Savior

In order to accomplish these goals, you will need to tell the Bible story clearly and, while doing so, emphasize the doctrinal themes important for evangelism.

These doctrinal themes are of great importance. Many Westerners are probably familiar with some of the Old Testament stories. But do they understand the points of doctrine which are embodied in the historical incidents recorded in the Bible?

Doctrinal themes

The doctrinal themes which are emphasized in this curriculum are those which will show people they are sinful, condemned, and helpless before God, their holy and righteous Creator and Judge. Also emphasized are those which will generate repentance and faith and bring complete dependence on the Lord Jesus Christ as the all-sufficient Savior.

The themes are constantly repeated throughout these lessons. This is the main strength of chronological teaching. The repetition of these themes is intentional because unbelievers are not usually immediately or easily gripped with the attributes of God, and most of all they don't readily see how **who God is** relates so importantly to them.

Themes about God

1. God is supreme and sovereign.

This is probably the most important, initial truth that people need to understand. That God is supreme, and therefore sovereign, is foundational to all other doctrines concerning God, and to all other spiritual matters. Before a person can be saved by trusting in Christ alone for his salvation, he must recognize that his sovereign Creator has the right to tell him what he should and should not do. He must come to grips with the fact that this sovereign One has the right to condemn him to everlasting punishment because of his disobedience.

The message of a sovereign God will cut against the grain of everything that has been taught to your students in our humanistic society. Man has exalted himself to a place of authority that belongs only to God. The message that God has ultimate authority because He is Creator will seem strange and foreign to your students, probably even irritating. But in the power of the Holy Spirit, the message of God's sovereignty will help your students realize that God has the right to hold each person accountable for his sin.

God's sovereign position is evidenced in the biblical record, and will be constantly emphasized throughout these lessons. For example, God showed His supremacy over Lucifer and the angels that rebelled against Him by removing them from their former positions in Heaven. Later, when Adam and Eve rebelled, God showed His sovereignty by removing them from the garden in Eden. Other significant demonstrations by God of these same attributes were in His dealings with Cain, the people in the days of Noah, and rebellious Pharaoh who dared to defy God by refusing to release the Israelites.

Through these lessons, your students will come to understand that God is supreme over Satan, man and all creation. His actions in history will reveal to them that He is always victorious, regardless of the strength or countless number of His adversaries. He overcomes all who oppose Him.

Your students will also learn that God is an active, living, present Person who is vitally interested in all that they are and do. They will come face to face with the truth that God is their almighty Creator and sovereign Judge to whom they will give account for everything they do and say.

2. God communicates with man.

God is not silent. He speaks to every person. As you teach these lessons, you will impress on your students not only that God has spoken but that He is still speaking. The Bible is not just a record of what God said to people in the past. It is also God's voice in the present.

While the lessons may not always state this truth, nevertheless, this is the emphasis of every lesson. God has spoken and is now speaking. If He is not speaking to us, there is little point in even considering the message of the Bible.

People in our society have the Bible literally at their fingertips. Yet the fact that God communicates with man through it has been largely ignored. People view the Bible as a good book, or as a book with philosophical nuggets, but most do not recognize it as the vehicle through which God communicates truth to man. Indeed, many claim that the Bible is not true. Nevertheless, God's Word stands clear, righteous and true, as it will for all eternity.

God is speaking in this day and age through Scripture, and He will speak to your students as they listen to His Word.

3. God is everywhere, all of the time. God knows everything.

These themes are embedded into every part of the story of the Bible (Hebrews 4:13). If taught correctly, these truths can be a powerful instrument in the hands of the Holy Spirit to bring deep conviction of sin. Until faced with the fact of God's constant presence and perfect knowledge of their every thought, word and action, most people are only concerned with keeping up appearances before their fellow man. Therefore, as Scripture says, *"There is no fear of God before their eyes"* (Romans 3:18).

Examples of God being there, seeing and knowing, are abundant in every Bible story. For example, the Lord saw that the wickedness of man was great in the earth in Noah's time, and God knew of Israel's plight as they toiled in slavery in Egypt. These points are great teaching opportunities, for through these events you will be able to impress on your students that **the God who was is the God who is**. God saw, and God sees. God knew, and God knows. No one can escape from this ever-present, all-seeing and all-knowing God (Psalm 139:1-18).

Be aware of what your students understand as you teach that God is everywhere, all of the time. They have probably been influenced by false teachings that God is everything and everything is God. God is everywhere, but He is not in everything; everything is not God. While the lessons make a clear distinction between the Creator God and His creation, you may need to reinforce this truth.

The theological terms "omnipresent" or "omniscient" are purposely not used in these lessons. It is important to keep the point clear and simple by avoiding terms which most unsaved people do not understand.

4. God is all-powerful.

That God is almighty and should therefore be worshiped and feared has little impact on godless, unbelieving mankind. That God is all-powerful is particularly difficult for people in our society to accept because they are in the habit of "scientifically proving" everything.

The theme of God's almighty power is clearly seen, not just in statements in the Bible but also in God's actions. His great power is seen in creation. It is also evident through His destruction of the human race by a global flood, in the obliteration of the cities of Sodom and Gomorrah, and in the devastation in Egypt through the plagues. The Lord said to Pharaoh, *"For this purpose I have raised you up, that I may show My power in you, and that My name may be declared in all the earth"* (Exodus 9:16).

Over and over again throughout the Old Testament, God demonstrated that He is unlimited in power. He opened the sea for the fleeing Israelites and provided their every need while they wandered for 40 years in the Arabian wilderness. God's power was also demonstrated through the Lord Jesus as He stilled the raging sea, instantly healed the sick, raised the dead, and fed 5000 people with just a few loaves and fishes.

When clearly expounded and applied to your unsaved hearers, the account of God's mighty power, demonstrated time and time again in Old Testament history and in the life of Christ, will be used by the Holy Spirit to humble their proud rebellious hearts and lead them to repentance.

The lessons do not use the word "omnipotent" because, as mentioned before, it is important to avoid using terminology that is unfamiliar to the unsaved.

5. God is holy and righteous. He demands death as the payment for sin.

We must teach that God Himself is the standard for goodness and, therefore, anything which disagrees with or is contrary to what He is, is sin. Anything less than what God is, is unacceptable to God.

Of all the truths about God, this one is most notably absent from today's "religious" thinking. Also missing from most preaching are messages about God's holiness, man's sinfulness and that death is the penalty for all sin. The initial message that unbelievers need to hear is not, "Smile, God loves you" – it is, *The soul who sins shall die"* (Ezekiel 18:4).

These lessons show God's holy and righteous character, as revealed in history by His consistent attitude of judgment on man's deviation from His holy standard. God will not overlook sin. All sin must be paid for. Furthermore, because God is righteous, He will never lower His standard of holiness nor accept anything less than the full, righteous payment for sin. Neither will God ever allow any man to approach Him unless the complete and righteous demands of His law are fully met.

Even though the righteous demands of God's law could only be provided through the blood of Jesus Christ, God still accepted sinners who came to Him in faith prior to Calvary, because Christ's death was, even then, a present reality to God (Revelation 13:8). During the Old Testament, however, worshipers had to be constantly reminded that their acceptance by God was not at the expense of justice. Death, the wages of sin, was constantly portrayed by the death of innocent animals.

Constant reference is made throughout the lessons to God's requirement of animal sacrifices, because these emphasized God's holiness and His just demand for the death of the sinner as the payment for sin. Animal blood could not be a replacement for the death of the sinner, but it was a constant reminder that nothing less than death could satisfy God's righteous demand (Hebrews 10:1-12).

6. God is loving, merciful and gracious.

God's love, mercy and grace shine most brightly against the dark backdrop of man's deliberate and constant rebellion. No sooner had Adam sinned by ignoring God's

clear command and warning, than God demonstrated His compassionate character. Because of His love, He exercised mercy by withholding the full judgment man justly deserved, and He exercised grace by promising a Savior and clothing naked, guilty man in the skins of animals killed by God Himself.

Demonstrations of God's love, mercy and grace are interwoven into every lesson in this curriculum. Even in the story of Sodom and Gomorrah, where God's wrath is so prominent, we see the portrayal of a merciful, loving and gracious God. God poured out vengeance, yet He delivered Lot.

Though while teaching the Old Testament, we will not tell of God's greatest demonstration of His love, mercy and grace which was through the death of His Son, we will constantly emphasize these glorious attributes of God. While faced with their sinfulness and a God who demands death as the payment for sin, your students will also have this hope – that they, too, may experience the love, mercy and grace of God.

7. God is faithful and does not change.

God never changes; therefore, His righteous standards never change, and He always keeps His promises. The lessons emphasize that God's attitude is always the same toward the proud and unrepentant, and that He is consistently merciful and faithful to forgive and save all who humble themselves and put their trust in the Lord Jesus..

Numerous opportunities are given throughout these lessons for you to emphasize that God remains the same as He was in the beginning and, therefore, He can be relied on to do all that He said He would. If there is the possibility that God will not carry out His threats of judgment on the unrepentant and not fulfill His promises of mercy for those who trust in Him, then the Bible stories have no application and are merely meaningless history of people long dead. But this is not so!

As you teach, you will be constantly impressing upon your hearers the truth that the God of the Bible has never changed and will not change in any of His attitudes and dealings with human beings. As He was in the past, so He is today. This emphasis will provide the student with truths which the Holy Spirit uses to produce conviction of sin, repentance towards God and then faith in God's promises of eternal life to all who put their faith in the Lord Jesus Christ.

Themes about man

1. Man is a sinner under the death penalty. He needs God and is helpless to save himself.

Man cannot please God by his own efforts. Only the grace of God can save him. These lessons establish that mankind's sinfulness before God began with Adam's disobedience to God (Roman 5:12). The sinfulness of man will be painfully obvious as you teach the biblical account of man's history.

During the lessons, you will remind your students repeatedly that they are helpless sinners under the death penalty and that only God can deliver them. Your students will undoubtedly chafe at the idea that they are helpless and cannot please God by their own efforts. People in our society are entrenched in the belief that mankind holds the solutions to all problems. Yet the simple truth is that only the grace of God can save sinners.

You will conclude these lessons with the wonderful and positive announcement that, just as God intervened to rescue believers throughout the Bible story, so today God rescues from death those who put their trust in the Savior, Jesus Christ.

2. Man can come to God only according to God's will and plan.

Because God is holy and supreme, He alone determines the way man can approach Him and be saved.

Whatever man does to approach God must be done exactly the way God has prescribed. This will be taught often throughout the Old Testament. After Adam and Eve sinned and realized they were naked, they made themselves aprons of leaves. God rejected their efforts to make themselves appear acceptable. If man was to be clothed acceptably before God, then it had to be done God's way. God took the initiative. He killed animals, made coats from their skins and put them on Adam and Eve. Later when Cain and Abel came to worship the Lord, Cain came according to his own way, which was unacceptable to God. Abel came by faith, which was acceptable. It had to be done God's way. This theme is also seen clearly in the building of the ark and of the Tabernacle.

You will emphasize this important principle of how God deals with all men so that your students will come to understand they cannot come to God according to their own ideas. They can only come to God through His appointed way – the Lord Jesus Christ (John 14:6).

3. Man must have faith in order to please God and be saved.

In Hebrews 11, the Holy Spirit guided the writer to list in chronological order many of the leading characters found throughout Old Testament history. The writer began with Abel and continued on to list Enoch, Noah, Abraham, Sarah, Isaac, Jacob, Joseph and Moses. Finally, knowing that those who could be mentioned are far too many, the writer concluded, *"... time would fail me to tell of Gideon and Barak and Samson and Jephthah, also of David and Samuel and the prophets"* (Hebrews 11:32).

As well as mentioning these people by name, the writer pointed out some of their most prominent accomplishments. For example, Abel offered a sacrifice that was acceptable to God. Enoch was taken to Heaven without dying. Noah built the ark. Abraham and Sarah left their home to live in a foreign country. Moses confronted Pharaoh with God's demands and rescued the Israelites. Later in the chapter, the writer listed some of the incredible exploits of yet other characters who lived towards the close of the Old Testament era. But as great as the accomplishments of all these people were, none of them were accepted by God because of the extraordinary feats they achieved. Faith in God was what made them acceptable to Him, for *"without faith it is impossible to please Him"* (Hebrews 11:6).

It is vitally important then that we, like the writer of Hebrews, keep the emphasis in each story on the faith of those whom God accepted. Even though the faith of the leading characters is not usually mentioned in the stories we will be teaching from the Old Testament, we will take our model from Hebrews 11. We will emphasize that it was faith in God, or the lack of faith in Him, that determined whether a person was ultimately accepted or rejected by God (Ephesians 2:8-9).

Themes about Satan

1. **Satan fights against God and His will. He is a liar and a deceiver. He hates man.**

   Satan and the angels who followed him in rebellion against God were created by God and, therefore, are subject to His authority. They are the implacable foes of God and man. Satan uses his angels and sinful man in his efforts to establish his own kingdom and to try to destroy the kingdom of God.

   Even though Satan and his angels are not often mentioned in the Old Testament

text, it is good to remind our hearers of their continual presence and influence in the history of mankind. We know from the New Testament that Satan is the *"god of this age"* (2 Corinthians 4:4) so we know he has always been present to tempt and guide men in their opposition to God and His will.

Even so, God was, and will always be, triumphant over every endeavor of Satan to destroy God's plans to bless His people and bring salvation to men.

Themes about Jesus Christ (New Testament only)

These are self-explanatory and are interwoven throughout the lessons on the Life of Christ.

1. **Jesus Christ is God.**

2. **Jesus Christ is man.**

3. **Jesus Christ is holy and righteous.**

4. **Jesus Christ is the only Savior.**

Keep a balance

We must beware lest we emphasize these doctrinal themes to such an extent that the biblical, historical account is forgotten or diminished. Both the historical stories and the doctrine taught by them are important.

If the stories are correctly told and expounded, they themselves will become a living, vibrant revelation of the doctrines which our hearers must know even when we do not specifically state the doctrine.

This is not to suggest that we should tell the stories uninterpreted, hoping that our hearers will understand from the biblical text what is so clear to us. As co-laborers together with God, we have been given the responsibility to expound and interpret the divine text and the recorded history. Like the Ethiopian eunuch, people need

Spirit-controlled "Philips" to make the scriptural interpretation clear. Keep a balance between storytelling and exposition so that one does not overshadow the other.

Now I "Get" It!

Hello; my name is Heather, and I would like to share with you how the *"Firm Foundations"* Bible study has impacted my life.

Before I had even heard about the study, I used to have an unhealthy view of God, and that view sometimes made me angry towards Him. It made me doubt His love and provision. I also had a big misconception about the Bible. I thought God gave it to us for the express purpose of telling us what to do and how to do it. And if I didn't, I'd better look out!

About a month before I came in contact with some missionaries who teach this curriculum, I had prayed, "God, I don't really know You, and I want to. I know a lot **about** You, but I don't really know what You are like."

Even though I was spiritually struggling, the first time I attended the *"Firm Foundations"* Bible study, I thought I was going to hear everything I already knew. After all, I'd gone to Bible college! Well, gladly, I was mistaken.

The very first lesson showed me that I had some misunderstandings which were hindering me from viewing God properly. Just in the first lesson, I found great hope – hope that God was going to clear all of my confusion. The Bible is **about** God, and the neat thing is that the Lord gave us the Bible so that we could learn to know Him. He is the central character in the Bible. It's not all about rules, "good" people, "bad" people, but rather about God Himself. I thought back to the Bible stories I'd heard as a child and realized that God was left out. Man was the hero, not God.

Prior to this study, I was getting a little truth here and a little truth there, and was somehow supposed to fit the puzzle together. The Bible wasn't meant to be studied like that. Starting in the beginning, it's easier to build precept upon precept, and then the Bible makes sense. Studying it in chronological order allows us to understand what God's purpose for man is. He wants to have a personal relationship with us. Isn't that amazing?

The Bible alone tells us what God thinks of us and what He sees as our greatest need. He gave us His Word so we can discover how great He is. What a loving God!

This study has slowly been changing my perspective about the character of God. I didn't really understand what He was like until I "saw" how He dealt with man in history past. My faith in Him is becoming more grounded. As I've seen the sinfulness of man compared to the absolute greatness of God and how He deals with us according to His justice, grace, mercy, love and holiness, it's almost more than my mind can fathom.

While this study's goal is intended to teach salvation, it is also helpful for those who have doubts about their salvation. Getting to know God on a more personal level gives a clearer understanding of salvation. These amazing and thought-provoking truths have really helped me, and I pray that they will help you too.

3

Preparing to Teach

Firm Foundations: Creation to Christ has been written and designed with the teacher in mind. You will find this course easy to study and easy to teach. But it does require taking the time to equip yourself before beginning because this curriculum's teaching approach is unique.

Read Part 1

Part 1 lays out the reasons why the Bible should be taught chronologically. It is vital that you understand and are convinced that the underlying reasons for this curriculum are based on biblical principles. Only then will you be able to teach with conviction and without rushing.

Read through the lessons

Ideally, you should read through the whole set of 48 lessons, along with the Scripture used in the context of the lessons. Doing so will give you a broad understanding of this method of teaching. It will also help you to become aware of what is covered and how the truths that you will introduce early in the lessons are expanded as you continue to teach.

Develop connection and credibility

Take the time to build bridges of friendships Be friendly. Be available to help. Listen. Live a faithful testimony. People will notice, and be more willing to listen to what you have to say, and think about their need to study God's Word.

Friendship Opens Opportunities

Our unsaved neighbors were no longer able to maintain their yard, so for a few years we trimmed their hedges and weeded as a gesture of friendship. As this couple's needs increased, we also helped with household chores and medical appointments.

Prior to all of this, we'd asked if these neighbors would like to study the Bible with us, but they had politely declined. However, after we'd demonstrated a personal interest in them, they agreed to study God's Word. Their explanation was, "We've seen you walk your talk."

By the end of the teaching sessions, both of them came to know Christ as their Savior.

– Paul

Be aware of what your audience believes

When we take the Gospel to the unsaved, whether to people previously exposed to the truth or to those who have not been exposed to the Bible, we must realize that we are not building on vacant land. Satan has had years to influence their hearts and minds with falsehood and misconceptions.

Your students will perceive what you teach according to what they already believe about the world and spiritual things. Even the terminology that you use may be misunderstood because they will interpret the words according to their own perception. So be aware that error has long been a part of your students' thinking.

When God Is Misunderstood

While teaching the very beginning lessons of this curriculum to a 17-year-old girl, she periodically interjected questions or comments that exposed her preconceived ideas about God.

"God is married to Mary, right?"

"I think God's really a pervert because He looks at us when we're naked."

These perceptions had been shaped by what she'd seen and heard at the movies.

We simply emphasized the authority of God's Word and assured her that as we got deeper into the studies, she would understand who He really is and what He is like.

As we taught about His character, this teen eventually exclaimed, "If I had not come to this Bible study, I wouldn't have understood who God is. I was really confused! So many of my questions have been answered."

– Pam

These lessons specifically target Western societies and already address what many Westerners believe or have heard. But before you teach, you should identify in the lessons any points that could clash with what your specific students believe.

I'm not suggesting you "attack" the students' beliefs, or even that you specifically point out to them that what they believe is false. Instead, bear in mind areas of potential misunderstanding and be ready to teach the truth clearly, **when appropriate in the lesson text.**

Don't get off track. Just keep teaching God's Word, staying alert to the issues which the students might misunderstand because of what they believe.

Identifying Confusion

In one group we taught, a student had grown up in a family that had certain religious beliefs. Although she did not agree with many aspects of that religion, her thinking had been strongly influenced by it.

Because we knew about her background, we were able to pinpoint portions of the lessons that would clash with what she thought, or places where there was potential for misunderstanding of terminology. Usually we just taught the point in the lesson, being careful to make sure all the students, not just her, really understood. As time went on, we were able to address the issues more directly, although never singling her out. For example, we would teach the emphasis of the lesson at hand, and then say something like, "Some religions teach such and such, but God's Word gives us the truth."

One day she exclaimed, "I'd always thought that the God of the Old Testament was the God of wrath and the God of the New Testament was the God of love. But that's not true. He's the same God."

By listening to the truth taught systematically and clearly, she understood.

– Ruth

Avoid creating an artificial religious atmosphere

The Holy Spirit only uses truth. The work and power of God are not dependent upon a man-made religious or spiritual climate. Jesus and the apostles spoke God's truth in normal, everyday situations. They did not create an artificial setting so people could "feel" God. They trusted in the power of the truth of the message they were speaking.

Gospel meetings traditionally open with a few hymns or choruses, a Bible reading, and a prayer. Although most Christians seem to think that this format is necessary for a successful meeting, we do not find it anywhere in Scripture. Of course, this does not immediately condemn such activities, but the fact remains that neither by a scriptural command nor by the example of the Lord Jesus or the apostles have we been guided in our evangelistic methods. They are purely traditional. While traditions are not necessarily wrong, our methods often cause misunderstanding and confusion in the minds of unsaved people.

For example, if your students have been taught the false gospel of salvation by works, they will associate being a Christian with religious activities. Therefore, they will think that participating in prayer and singing during your teaching sessions will help to make them acceptable to God.

Don't lead the unsaved in prayer

Traditionally, in most evangelistic meetings, someone will lead in prayer. In essence, they are inviting unsaved people to join with the saved in praying to God. This is unscriptural! *"The sacrifice of the wicked is an abomination to the Lord, but the prayer of the upright is His delight"* (Proverbs 15:8). *"One who turns away his ear from hearing the law, even his prayer is an abomination"* (Proverbs 28:9). When evangelizing, neither Jesus nor the apostles were ever recorded as having prayed with unsaved people.

The Lord Jesus said, *"No one comes to the Father except through Me"* (John 14:6). Prayer

---

Don't Mix the Message

The couple across the street from us had been churched as young people but had avoided "religion" as adults. However, they viewed us as religious simply because we attended Sunday services and taught Bible studies.

When they saw the change in other neighbors who had become believers while attending our home Bible study, this couple decided they, too, wanted to study God's Word. However, since they were unbelievers, we felt it wise to have a separate study for them. We made it a point to avoid any Christian practices such as prayer time, which might inadvertently introduce salvation through "works." Rather, we spent a bit of time before each lesson chatting about the day's events, and ended the sessions with some type of dessert, then a good-bye hug.

When this couple came to know Christ as their Savior, the husband exclaimed that he'd always thought that he'd had to "do" something to be saved. He rejoiced that Jesus had done all that was necessary for him.

It was not long at all before prayer became a "natural" part of their lives as believers. The *Firm Foundations: Creation to Christ* study helps teachers to avoid putting the "cart before the horse."

– Rasmussens

---

must be in Jesus' name. When believers pray, they *"enter the Holiest by the blood of Jesus"* (Hebrews 10:19). Unbelievers cannot come to God in Jesus' name, nor do the children of God have the power to bring the children of Satan along with them into God's holy presence. The unsaved must be taught that because of their sin, they are shut out from the presence of God, and that only through Christ and His death can they be forgiven of their sins and be reconciled to God. How can we invite them to pray with us before they believe and are reconciled?

If your students have gone to church, they may expect you to pray before your sessions. For unbelievers, however, prayer is essentially a formula.

Praying is commonly used by Satan to make unsaved people feel, and therefore believe, that they are accepted by God. In spite of the impossibility of unbelievers entering God's presence by prayer, some Christians even encourage them to pray before they are saved. This actually hinders people from facing their great need of true godly repentance and accepting Christ's saving work on their behalf.

Be careful not to create false security

Those who do not see the seriousness of the issues involved will probably think that this is merely splitting hairs. Those, however, who are aware of the false security which prayer and singing have given millions throughout the organized church worldwide will readily agree that these matters need to be carefully considered. Anything done in Christian service which Satan may use to make people feel accepted by God, and, therefore, hinder them from facing the reality of their lost condition, would be best eliminated from our evangelistic methods.

An example from the mission field will illustrate what I'm talking about.

Some young Palawano men were conducting an evangelistic outreach from their local church to a village of unsaved people. These young evangelists were welcomed every week by the unsaved people of this village. The people gladly sang the hymns and joined in prayer and the reading of the Scriptures. They listened attentively to the Gospel messages, but there was no evidence of repentance. No one made a verbal profession of faith in Christ alone as their hope of salvation.

The young Christian evangelists didn't know what to do. These unsaved people seemed happy and secure. Their spiritual eyes were blind to their need for spiritual sight because they believed they could already see (John 9:40-41). They thought

of themselves as already "in God." (This term was used continually by unsaved religionists in Palawan.)

One day, the young men who were conducting these meetings asked for my advice. I encouraged them to discontinue all singing and praying in their meetings because I knew that the majority of the people were trusting that God would accept them because they did these things.

When the young men first considered this suggestion of eliminating all singing and praying from their evangelistic meetings, they were confused. They wondered how they could conduct meetings without these activities. All Gospel meetings they had previously attended followed the pattern modeled by the previous missionaries with singing and praying.

From the Scriptures, I explained to the young men that their responsibility was to simply teach the Word of God to the unsaved and that singing and praying should only be included in meetings of the children of God. I told them, "Just gather the people together and teach them God's Word. This is what Jesus and the apostles did whenever they taught. They did not first ask the people to sing and join together in prayer."

I also advised these men to temporarily withhold the Gospel. I explained, "The unsaved people you are teaching have heard the Gospel many times, but it has never meant much to them. They are quite satisfied to go through the form of meeting, singing, praying, and listening to the message because this makes them feel they are accepted by God. What they need at this stage is to be taught about God's holiness, about what His Law requires sinners to do if they are to be pleasing to God, and about their own sinfulness and inability to perfectly obey all the words of God. They must be prepared in this way; otherwise, they will not see their need for the Lord Jesus and the Gospel."

As I talked with these young men, they understood the reasons for omitting singing and praying from the meeting. The next time they visited the village, they deliberately left their hymnbooks at home. When they met with the people, they read God's Word and then continued immediately teaching the people, emphasizing the holy and righteous character of God and the need for everyone to repent – that is, to agree with God that they were sinners and were justly condemned.

Just after the men began to teach, some of the people interrupted and asked, "Aren't we going to sing and pray?"

"No, we are not," the young men answered. Then they explained why they had decided not to sing and pray anymore in the evangelistic meetings. They told the people, "God has never asked Satan's children to sing about Him. God doesn't accept the singing of those who are not His children. He tells only His own children to sing praises to Him. (See Ephesians 5:18-20.)

"Neither does God ask you to pray to Him. You cannot come to God and talk to Him, because your sins are still between you and God. (See Isaiah 59:1-2; Ephesians 2:11-13.) We prayed for you before we left our village, and the believers in our place are also praying that you will realize that you are sinners who can never please God."

In response, these unsaved people asked, "What then does God want us to do?"

"Just listen to and take notice of God's message to you in His Word," was the reply given.

What was the result of this different approach? Because the people were stripped of the religious activities in which they had previously trusted, they were startled into a realization of their lost condition before God.

Just as in that situation, we need to realize that traditional methods can actually lead people to Hell.

Christians were not sent into the world with rituals. We were sent with the message of God's Word. God has *committed to us the word of*

reconciliation" (2 Corinthians 5:19), and that is all we need.

Recognize the importance of avoiding religious terminology

Much religious terminology is meaningless to the unsaved. That is why we have avoided religious terms in this curriculum, and when words such as "born again," "faith," "repent" are used, they are first carefully introduced. So as you teach, avoid terms that will be confusing.

Say It Right

One of the women in our Bible study initially came to us spiritually confused. Even though we were not delving into the Gospel at that point in time, she was anxious, focused on and tormented about one thing – the fear of not knowing if she was a Christian or not. Early on, she e-mailed me the following:

"I get confused when I hear people say, 'Trust Jesus to save you,' like it depends upon my trusting to get Jesus to save me. I have heard other people say, 'Once you have trusted in Jesus, you can be sure that your sins are paid for,' like my trusting Jesus gets Him to pay for my sins. That is when faith feels like work to me, because somehow it depends on me to get Jesus' attention by my faith.

"I consistently look at myself, wondering if I have truly believed. … I hear preachers say that there is a 'head' faith and a 'heart' faith. It makes believing on Christ seem to be a special kind of faith. … My mind gets awfully confused with the play on words that people use. … God sounds awfully hard to find."

We encouraged this lady to just keep attending our teaching sessions because much of this turmoil would be put to rest as she learned God's message progressively and clearly revealed in the Bible. We were careful to steer clear of the terminology that had been so problematic to her in the past.

I love the way this curriculum presents the Gospel in total simplicity – the way it's meant to be shared with others. It's truly freeing to those who are confused.   – Pam

---

4

Teaching the Lessons

These Bible lessons cover key Scriptures and emphasize the truths necessary for evangelism. This curriculum is appropriate for any audience – home groups or church groups – and for any size audience – one-on-one or large gatherings.

Dialogue teaching style

Not only do the chronological Bible lessons show what to teach, they also show how to teach. On a number of occasions when I was conducting seminars, missionaries requested that I teach the lessons to them as if they were tribal people, so I could demonstrate my teaching style. Subsequently, I wrote the original lessons as though I were actually addressing a group of tribal people in Palawan, an island of the Philippines. When we adapted those lessons for this book, we kept the same pattern, but applied them to a Western audience.

I deliberately used dialogue approach. Throughout the lessons, you will see that I constantly encourage the people to think about something or to respond to a question. It is important that we do not preach but rather teach. Your style should not be stiff and stilted but lucid, free and spontaneous.

There are many benefits for when your students ask and answer questions, discuss the Scriptures being taught, and express their views. By maintaining a dialogue approach, you will find that the class participants' interest level will be higher; they will be more relaxed, and they will learn more quickly.

Authoritative evangelism

There is a common form of Bible study where each person gives his own ideas about the portion of Scripture under consideration, and then the leader summarizes the different thoughts and interpretations given by those present. This is not what I am suggesting when advocating a dialogue approach. Any method of teaching which fails to give authoritative answers from the Word of God, is not biblical.

Anyone who teaches God's Word is to speak as God's ambassador, not as one who binds peoples' consciences to him or his interpretation. He must present the Scriptures as the final authority. Many people today do not believe there is absolute truth. This curriculum's lessons constantly reaffirm that God's Word is the only reliable source of spiritual truth, and the way you teach should reinforce that as well.

These lessons in this study are directed, with the teacher taking the lead role by systematically teaching the lesson and keeping any discussion on track. Though there is plenty of opportunity for student comment and interaction, these lessons are not intended to be taught in a discussion format.

Maintain a balance between allowing students to freely express themselves and having an authoritative ministry in the power of the Holy Spirit which declares God's truth regardless of what anyone says or thinks (1 Thessalonians 1:5; 2:4-5).

The Bible – the sole authority

One way in which you can emphasize that you are not the authority, and that all your knowledge of spiritual things comes only from the Bible, is to always teach from your open Bible. Your students need to see that you are, indeed, teaching God's Word.

Don't rush

Faith comes through hearing the Word of God (Romans 10:17). "To hear" in the scriptural sense is also "to understand." As teachers, we are responsible to make certain our hearers clearly understand what they are being taught.

Be sure your listeners are logically thinking through each point with you. These lessons are written in a way that will help you appeal to your students to think through each new concept.

Make it interesting

You cannot teach people unless you have their attention. Stimulate your students' minds by using the illustration and participation questions in the lessons. Make sure they are actively thinking along with you while you are teaching. Proceed with calculative precision, helping establish each point firmly in their minds.

Use illustrations

The Lord Jesus Christ, the perfect Teacher, used common everyday objects, situations and human relationships to illustrate divine truths. His stories, illustrations and parables were taken from the normal, cultural experiences of His hearers – from fishermen to farmers, fathers to sons, servants to kings. He used natural and commonly seen objects, such as lilies, grass, bread and sheep, to illuminate His hearers' understanding and to help them discern spiritual things unseen by the natural eye.

We, too, should use objects, real stories, and normal, everyday situations to explain and emphasize the meaning of spiritual truths in the Scriptures. For this reason, I have included illustrations in the lesson text. Each one is preceded by a teacher's note, explaining the point of the illustration.

You will find that most of them can be used as written or with only minor adjustments. Adapt as needed to make them meaningful to your hearers.

Keep to the subject

One of the most important jobs for the teacher is to keep the class on track. This is especially true in our society where people have a penchant for discussion. It is your job to keep the lesson progressing.

Always hold the central topic clearly before your hearers. Don't get drawn into subjects or details which come later in the Scriptures. Avoid these distractions with a statement such as: "That is a very good question, but since we will be covering the answer in an upcoming lesson, I'd rather not jump ahead."

Build patiently

Some Bible teachers find it very difficult to follow the biblical principle of progressive teaching. In their eagerness for people to know all the truth, these teachers forget the necessity of first laying foundations and then building, step-by-step. They find it extremely uncomfortable to leave people temporarily ignorant of important truth which will be taught later.

Teaching is like building. Both take time. A building is completed brick by brick, plank by plank, story by story, according to the plans of the building architect. Time must be given for concrete to harden, bonding to seal and paints to dry before the builder can proceed with the next stage of construction.

It is important not to crowd all the long-term goals into each lesson. Every story told should move the hearers forward another step in their understanding of the complete story of the Bible and body of doctrinal truth.

Begin with questions

In order to tie every new segment of the story back to the portion already taught, each lesson begins with review questions.

These questions have a two-fold purpose: They remind the students of the previous story and the doctrinal truths taught through it, as well as provide the basis and introduction for the coming story. This time of review also allows the teacher an opportunity to clear up any misunderstandings about what has already been taught before proceeding to the next part of the story.

Continue with questions

Interaction during the lesson will help to keep your students alert and will give you feedback regarding what is really being communicated. As individuals respond to your questions, not only does it give them an opportunity to express their views but it also gives you the opportunity to see what they really believe.

Questions are interspersed throughout the lessons. Use them to cause those you are teaching to carefully ponder the truths they are hearing.

Be aware that you need to pause after asking questions so as to allow students to answer. After they have responded, you can follow up with further explanation from the lesson text.

Each question in the lesson is followed by an expected answer. You will find that someone may give a very good answer which is different from the one in the text. That's fine because it shows the students are thinking through the truths. Agree with a reasonable answer, and then rephrase the question so that someone will give the desired answer for that particular question.

Through questioning, you are teaching your students to look carefully at the story to learn what God wants them to know about Himself, themselves, Satan and the Lord Jesus.

Tips for questioning

1. Allow your students to answer in their own words.

2. Give them time to think and to discuss important points.

3. Show respect by listening to what they say.

4. Address some questions to the whole group, and others directly to individuals. Try to involve every person.

5. Do not grill them. The question time should not cause embarrassment.

6. If students are unable to reply, or if their answer is incorrect, ask them other questions which may remind them of the correct answer.

7. Commend them for correct answers, the part they remembered, or for anything they say which is helpful.

8. Give the correct answer as specified in the lesson.

9. When necessary, explain the answer in greater detail

Handling students' questions

When you begin teaching the Scriptures, your students may have misunderstandings about who God is, where He is, what He does, etc. Do not be concerned and don't try to correct them all at once. Continue to teach *"precept upon precept, line upon line, ... here a little, there a little"* (Isaiah 28:10). Their knowledge of God will grow through the unfolding historical drama, because this is the way God has chosen to reveal Himself. Continue to teach God's Word carefully and prayerfully, trusting the Lord to make Himself known in all His glory through the Scriptures.

People in our society have been bombarded with the media's passion for asking "the hard questions." It seems to be a cultural sport to make a leader sweat under a barrage of difficult questions. Don't allow yourself to be pressured into answering things that don't pertain to the subject.

When faced with a tough question that is valid but seems unanswerable, remind the student of what has already been taught about the unchangeable character of God and the truth of His Word. It may be necessary to explain that there are some things that God has not chosen to reveal to us.

Don't force agreement

Although we should make the message meaningful to students by asking pointed questions, it is usually unwise to ask them if they accept and truly believe what they are being taught. This is especially true early in the teaching program. Questions of this nature may force people into a premature decision. They may reject or accept the Bible before they really understand its message.

The teacher should just faithfully teach the Word, allowing time for it to take root and grow under the direction of the Holy Spirit. Human efforts that try to force the new birth result in mere professions of faith without true possession of the life of God. Only God can bring a soul to understanding and salvation (1 Corinthians 3:7).

This doesn't mean that we shouldn't exhort people to accept the truth, repent, and believe the Gospel. This, too, is the responsibility of the faithful servant of Christ. In most situations, however, it is unwise to force people to answer to a human being. The teacher's responsibility is to help people realize that they are accountable to God and must answer to Him.

If students contradict what you teach them from God's Word, ask them what God says about the subject. The issue is between them and God, not between them and you.

Read the Scriptures

As stated earlier, each lesson should be taught with an open Bible. The verses should be read, either by you or by your students. Do not merely tell the narrative in your own words.

I believe that the reading of the Scriptures is tantamount to "teaching." If the Scriptures have been read, then the truth has been taught. You still need to explain it and reinforce it, but actually reading the Scripture is a vital part of teaching the Word.

A major mistake that is made constantly from the pulpit and in the Sunday school class is that the reading of the Scriptures is not viewed as the first important part of the learning process. This is why the reading is often hurried or unclear. And because people don't think of the reading of the Scriptures as teaching, they read the passage and then retell it in their own words. It is as though God's Word is not as valuable as them saying it. As a result, the hearers are not taught to listen carefully to the reading. They learn to rely on what the preacher or teacher says instead of what they heard read from the Scriptures. They don't judge the teaching by the Word. One of my

Scripture Version in this Curriculum

This curriculum uses NKJV as the Scripture base. It would be fine to use another version provided it faithfully spells out the meaning of the original Scriptures.

On occasion, a portion of a verse will be quoted in the lesson text to avoid getting into themes not pertinent to evangelism. If you are using a different version than the one used in these lessons, you will find the wording will be different in these quoted texts. Many Hebrew and Greek words have multiple meanings that overlap, and different versions use different words. If you examine the verse carefully, however, you will find each is saying the same thing. That is, the truth is there in whichever Bible version you use, and it is those truths you are teaching.

criteria in writing and teaching is to try to show the importance of listening to God's Word being read.

Our responsibility is to teach the Word of God. Verse-by-verse exposition of the Scriptures is the best way to do this. In the lessons, I have indicated to the teacher which verses are to be read and when to read them.

It is unwise to read the whole section of Scripture which will be taught in the lesson before beginning to teach. If you read the whole story before teaching, the story will hold no surprises for your audience. One of the most important elements in the art of storytelling is suspense, so maintain an air of excitement and anticipation, keeping your hearers looking forward to what comes next.

While each story told will have its high point, each lesson is yet another step toward the final climax of the story of redemption. The story of redemption begins in Genesis 3:15 and finds its fulfillment and culmination in the death, burial, and resurrection of the Lord Jesus Christ. Teach the Scriptures as one story, even though you are presenting it in individual lessons.

Teaching Messianic prophecies

The Old Testament Scriptures find their fulfillment in Christ (John 1:45; Luke 24:44-46). The Old Testament is like a signpost, continually pointing forward to the coming Redeemer. Just as the Old Testament believers looked forward to the coming of the Deliverer, teach so your hearers will be anticipating the Savior's coming.

The Old Testament contains many prophecies about the coming Deliverer. However, the Old Testament does not record His name or title. Therefore, as we teach, we will not mention the fulfillment of the prophecies, nor will we refer to the coming Deliverer by His given name or titles – the Lord Jesus Christ. Instead, we will not reveal who He is until we reach the revelation of His person and work in the New Testament.

Students in this society will undoubtedly recognize that "the Deliverer" is Jesus. If they mention it, simply acknowledge that this is true. But then explain that because you are teaching the Bible chronologically in its historical sequence, you will use the term "the Deliverer" since it wasn't known before His birth that the coming Savior would be called "Jesus."

In the New Testament lessons, you will be directed to point back to the Old Testament and remind your hearers of the prophecies which pointed forward and are completely fulfilled in Christ. In this way, we will interpret the Old Testament by the New Testament according to the way chosen and revealed by the Holy Spirit.

In Figure 4-1, I have given Genesis 3:15 as an example of the way we will teach all the Old Testament prophecies. This promise is regarding the seed of the woman who will come and bruise the head of the serpent. When teaching this verse, we will tell our hearers that this promise will be fulfilled by the coming Deliverer, but we will not disclose His identity by using His earthly name

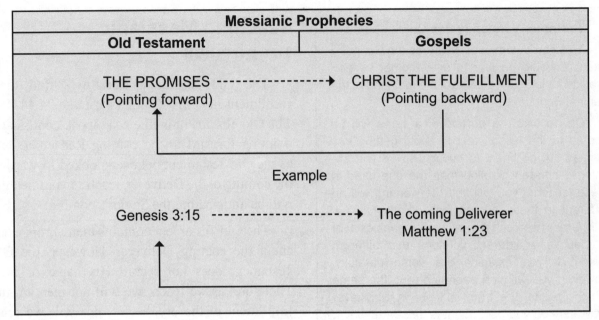

Figure 4-1

and titles. In addition, we will not read the actual fulfillment in Matthew 1:23. Later in the teaching program, when we teach Matthew 1:23, we will then point back and remind our hearers of the promise given in Genesis 3:15, and emphasize the faithfulness of God in keeping His Word.

Teaching Messianic types

When teaching Messianic types in the Old Testament, we will not point forward to Jesus because there is no indication in the Old Testament Scriptures that these types are actually foreshadowing Him.

As an example, see Figure 4-2. The manna is clearly a type of Christ. However, when teaching about the manna in the Old Testament, we will not point forward and say that a Savior is coming, who, like the manna, will provide spiritual food for all who put their trust in Him. We will simply teach the story and the details relating to the manna in preparation for the time when we teach from the New Testament that Jesus is the only spiritual food to give eternal life. From John 6:32, we will point back and remind our students of the details concerning the manna in Exodus 16:14-15.

Adding New Testament information

Throughout the Old Testament lessons, I have included some details and information which are not included in the Old Testament Scripture text. These additions, gleaned from the New Testament, throw more light on the story and give a better and more instructive interpretation of the words and actions of the characters and, therefore, of what actually took place in the Old Testament story.

For example, although Genesis 4:4 does not tell us that Abel came to God by faith, Hebrews 11:4 does. By including the information from Hebrews 11:4, we can correctly interpret the actions of Abel in our exposition of Genesis 4. In addition, in 1 John 3:12, we are told that Cain *"was of the wicked one and murdered his brother."* On the basis of this Scripture, we may inform our hearers that Satan led Cain to murder Abel.

It is unnecessary to inform the listeners where these added details are found in the Scriptures, unless they specifically ask. The added details

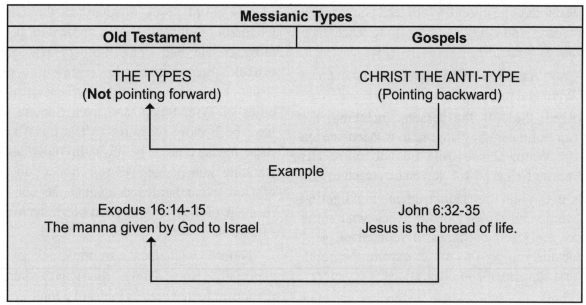

Figure 4-2

are interwoven into the story as part of the exposition.

For the teacher's sake, however, I have included cross-references so you will know where the information is found in the New Testament. These verification verses are given only for your instruction and should not be read to the students. That is difficult to do in our society because your students will want proof. So, if you feel it necessary to share these passages with the students, be aware that most contain topics and themes that you are not covering in these evangelism lessons. Don't get pulled off into teaching from these passages. You can remind the class that many portions of Scripture deal with numerous themes, but that you want to stick to the point at hand.

When to present the Gospel

These lessons follow the progressive revelation of scriptural truth, and it is good during your class time to follow this plan through to the completion of the course.

But individual students may be ready at any time to hear the Gospel. You do not know how much previous teaching they have had, nor do you know what the Holy Spirit has been doing in their hearts. While it is best not to present the Gospel to the class until you teach about Jesus' death, burial and resurrection in Lesson 47, you should always be ready to share the Gospel individually with any of your students.

When presenting the Gospel, avoid confusing religious terminology and jargon that's unfamiliar to your students. We commonly hear the phrase, "ask Jesus to come into your heart," "receive Christ," "get saved," or even "go forward." The message is much clearer when we say, "Believe that Jesus shed His blood and died on the Cross to make full payment for your sins. He took on Himself the punishment you deserve. Therefore, put your faith in Him alone as your Savior."

Putting it all together

Paul wrote to Timothy, *"Be diligent to present yourself approved to God, a worker who does not need to be ashamed, rightly dividing the word of truth"* (2 Timothy 2:15).

The following checklist will lead you through the steps as you study and prepare to teach each lesson.

❑ Pray. Ask God to help you understand His Word and these lessons.

❑ Read through the lesson, including the Scriptures as they appear in it. Meditate on the Word, and ask the Lord to make His message clear to you so you can teach it.

❑ Go through the lesson again, highlighting words and phrases that will jog your mind as you teach. Jot notes to yourself of other details you plan to use to expand the point, and adjustments to illustrations.

❑ Think of the possible responses of your students, and ask the Lord to help you to know how to best handle their comments and questions. Make notes of how you will answer them.

❑ Pray daily for your students.

Use the outline and your highlighting as a framework to keep you on track as you teach.

Does this sound like a lot of work? It is. But it's worth it. You will never regret the time you spend preparing and teaching these lessons. It will pay off in your own life, in the classroom, and in the lives of your students – for all eternity.

Handling little or no response

The initial response to the climax of teaching chronologically has usually been remarkable. Thousands of people throughout the world have been enlightened as they have come to understand their sinfulness and helplessness to save themselves and have, subsequently, put their faith in the Lord Jesus Christ as their Savior.

But there are places where there has been little or no response. Just as soils differ greatly in yielding crops, even though given the same care, cultivation and seed, so, too, individuals, families and groups will differ in their receptivity and response to the Scriptures.

The Lord Jesus condemned the cities of Chorazin, Bethsaida and Capernaum because, although He had done most of His greatest miracles before them, they refused to repent. Jesus clearly indicated that the heathen Gentile cities of Tyre, Sidon, and even Sodom, would have been more receptive to His ministry than these Jewish cities. The Jews, through their long-standing knowledge, yet rejection of the truth of God, were hardened against the convicting message of their long-awaited Messiah (Matthew 11:20-24).

Numerous incidents in the book of Acts, especially from Paul's missionary journeys, demonstrate that some groups of people are more receptive and open to the Word of God than others. One outstanding example is the attitude of the Jews in Berea compared to the Jews in Thessalonica. *"These were more fair-minded than those in Thessalonica, in that they received the word with all readiness, and searched the Scriptures daily to find out whether these things were so"* (Acts 17:11).

God knows beforehand whether or not people will receive His message and, in spite of this, He still sends His servants to preach His Word. So what do you do if the students God has given to you seem disinterested and unreceptive?

You first need to remember that only God can change their hearts. You also need to remember that the students are accountable to God for their own responses. Your responsibility is not to change them, but to teach clearly and consistently.

Examine the way you teach

If people are not responding, you may need to make some adjustments to the way you teach. It will help to think through the following questions.

• Are you doing all you can to develop and maintain connection and credibility with your students? Do you have a quality relationship with them? Do they look upon you as a friend and one from whom they might learn?

- Are the Scriptures coming across to your students like mere ancient history, quite apart from their present reality? Are you consistently applying the message specifically to your students so that they will realize that God's Word is speaking to them personally?

- Are they impressed by the nature and character of God exemplified in the stories? If they haven't begun to fear God and to judge their sin in the light of His holiness and righteousness, is it because you are covering the material too quickly?

- Do their previous misconceptions about God and His Word hinder them from understanding or accepting the Bible message? Are you clearly addressing their misunderstanding?

- Do you vary the pace of your lesson presentations? Are your students constantly alert, wondering what is coming next?

- Is your teaching style interesting? Are you animated, expressive and imaginative?

- Are the students able to focus on the key points of the lessons? Do you reign in disruptions and direct discussion?

- Does the message of the Bible grip and excite you personally? If it does not excite you, you will not be able to teach in an enthusiastic, joyful and vibrant manner, and your students will not be gripped by the reality and wonder of God's message to the world.

- Do you foster interaction as you teach by asking questions, by allowing your students to ask you questions, and by giving the opportunity for comments and discussion?

- Are you finding out if individuals are appropriating the fundamental truths relating to their position as sinners before God? Teaching does not need to be limited to a public meeting. Talk with students in other venues to make sure they see that God is speaking to them personally through His Word.

- Are there hindrances in your life which may be hindering the work of the Holy Spirit through you as His instrument? (See 1 Peter 3:7.)

- Are you depending on the Lord? You may think, "It's my fault because I don't really know how to teach." Or you may think, "I'm a born teacher, so the problem must be in the curriculum." Either attitude evidences dependence on your own ability and not dependence on God.

- Are you being faithful in praying that the Holy Spirit will make God's Word clear to your students? While methods and techniques are important, we must not depend on them to prepare, convict, and lead people to the Savior, but rather on the presence and power of the Holy Spirit.

Starting over

If you teach through this curriculum and don't see unbelievers respond to God's offer of salvation, keep in mind that it's not the chronological teaching approach that is a problem. Truth still remains truth, even if there is no response.

Although people generally do recognize their need of the Savior after such a clear and simple presentation of God's Word, it's possible that some may have clearly understood and come under the conviction of the Holy Spirit, yet deliberately refused what they were taught (Acts 7:51-54). Or they still may not have understood and need to hear the teaching again.

If they will allow you the opportunity to begin again in Genesis and teach the material once more, trust the Lord to eventually bring spiritual understanding, heart conviction and salvation. Some teachers have found that their students only recognized truth after hearing the complete teaching a second or third time.

However, it's important to remember that whether or not you actually see fruit of your labor, nothing done for the Lord, in accordance with His Word and in fellowship with the Holy Spirit, is wasted time or effort.

5

Teaching Aids

Used wisely and at the appropriate time, visual teaching aids will have great impact in assisting your students to understand the Word of God.

Seeing Leads to Understanding

One of the ladies who attended our chronological Bible study used to joke about needing to see it to understand it. She was a visual learner.

So for her benefit, we used visual aids frequently. And it certainly was worth it. Not only did it help her, but others in the class also appreciated seeing the truth as well as hearing it. They almost always copied the visuals down in their notebooks.

– Ruth

Included with this set of lessons are visuals which were specifically designed to be used with this curriculum.

Maps

This set of three 16½ x 21½ maps (Figure 5 - 1) cover the key locations which you will be teaching about in the lessons.

I have suggested in teacher instruction notes when to point to locations on the maps.

Figure 5-1

Chronological Time Line

This time line (Figure 5 - 2) highlights the characters and events covered in this course. It is not intended to be an exhaustive chronology. Once introduced, it would be helpful to keep it always on display.

I have suggested in teacher instruction notes when to point to the names and events on the Chronological Time Line.

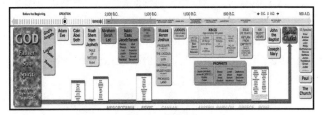

Figure 5-2

Prophecy Chart

This chart (Figure 5 - 3) lists Old Testament prophecies concerning Christ. Instructions tell you when to point to it. Once it has been introduced in Lesson 30, it should always be on display.

Figure 5-4

Pictures

NTM has developed a set of pictures designed to be used with the chronological teaching program. A few of those pictures, representing key events, are included as posters with the supplemental visual aids that come with this curriculum, but not all are. The full set of NTM's chronological pictures in various sizes is available separately should you wish to use it. (Figure 5 - 5)

What God Said Would Happen to
The Deliverer

	Prophecy	Fulfillment
Isaiah 9:7	Be David's descendant	Matthew 1:1
Isaiah 7:14	Be born of a virgin	Matthew 1:22-23
Micah 5:2	Be born in Bethlehem	Matthew 2:1
Hosea 11:1	Be brought out of Egypt	Matthew 2:14-15
Isaiah 11:2	Some of His characteristics	Luke 2:52
Isaiah 53:4-5	Suffer for others	John 10:11
Zechariah 9:9	Enter Jerusalem on a colt	Mark 11:7
Psalm 41:9	Be betrayed by a friend	Mark 14:10
Zechariah 11:12-13	Be sold for 30 pieces of silver	Matthew 26:14-15
Psalm 27:12	Be accused by false witnesses	Mark 14:56-57
Isaiah 50:6	Be struck and spit upon	Mark 14:65
Isaiah 53:7	Be silent when accused	Mark 15:3-5
Isaiah 53:3	Be rejected by Jews	Mark 15:9-14
Psalm 69:4	Be hated without cause	Mark 15:10
Psalm 22:16	His hands and feet pierced	Mark 15:24
Psalm 22:18	His clothing gambled for	Mark 15:24
Isaiah 53:12	Die with the wicked	Mark 15:27
Psalm 22:6-8	Mocked and insulted	Mark 15:29-32
Isaiah 53:9	Be buried with the rich	Mark 15:43-46
Psalm 16:10	Rise again	Mark 16:6
Psalm 68:18	Go back to Heaven	Acts 1:9

Figure 5-3

Posters

Attractive posters (Figure 5 - 4) have been specifically created to enhance your teaching. These posters will add interest to your teaching, and be particularly helpful for students who learn best visually.

Cues in the lesson text will tell you when to present these supplemental visuals.

Figure 5-5

Other pictures are available commercially. If you choose to use them, be sure they are biblical in content, because some are not. For example, a Bible picture might show large animals sitting on the deck of Noah's ark, when we know they were likely much smaller in size and were below deck. Bible pictures should be realistic and according to Scripture.

Student notebook

This optional notebook includes space for the students to write key points during class as you teach the lesson. Each notebook lesson also contains questions for personal study and review after class. (See Figure 5 - 6)

Figure 5-6

DVD

A PowerPoint-type presentation of the key points for each lesson is located on the DVD that comes with the lessons. This will be helpful for students as they take notes, and will aid you in keeping the class on track.

The DVD also includes the chronological maps, time line and other supplemental visuals.

Figure 5-7

Order information

- **Australia:** books_aus@ntm.org **or** 07.3208.9634

- **Canada:** www.ntmc.ca **or** bookstore@ntmc.ca **or** 519.369.2622

- **United Kingdom:** http://uk.ntm.org/shop **or** books@ntm.org.uk **or** 44.1472.387700

- **USA:** www.ntmbooks.com **or** books@ntm.org **or** 800.321.5375